Weaving The Values of My Heritage for My Best Life

Weaving the Values
Of My Heritage
for My Best Life

This Lifebook is not intended as a substitute for the medical advice of physicians or other health professionals. The reader should regularly consult a physician in matters relating to his/her health and particularly with respect to any symptoms that may require diagnosis or medical attention.

© by Sagesse Life Promotions
To request permissions contact
ordering@sagesslife.com
First Edition February 2021

All rights reserved. No part of this publication may be reproduced or transmitted in any form or by any means, electronic or mechanical, including photocopying, recording, or any other information storage and retrieval system, without the written permission of the publisher.

Internet addresses given in this book were accurate at the time it went to press.

Printed in the United States of America

Published in Hellertown, PA

Cover and interior design and illustrations by Georgia Wilson with Adobe Images

Library of Congress Control Number 2020925569

ISBN #978-1-950459-28-5
2 4 6 8 10 9 7 5 3 1 paperback

www.MomosaPublishing.com

*I am so very happy that you have chosen
Weaving the Values of My Heritage
for My Best Life!*

This Heritage Lifebook is the first book in a series
of four, which I hope you will find very useful.
The sage teachings of our rich African heritage
are expressed in Adinkra symbols
to build a solid foundation for telling your story
and decision-making.

In this African Heritage Lifebook, you will determine
seven core values to fill your "Basket of Abundance"
with those personal attributes,
which you treasure and will use to live your best life.

Knowing, growing, and using these attributes
with them being the center of who you are
and how you want to represent yourself to others,
inspires a feeling of high self-esteem.

Appreciating your value creates an internal environment
where personal growth is most successful.
These values are living and transform as you grow.

Opening yourself to possibilities
makes you eagerly want to live your best,
and success becomes a limitless part of you.

The other Heritage Lifebooks use the
strong foundation that you have built
to set life plans with effective goals
for your spiritual, mental, and physical health
and bring those plans to fruition.

Georgia

Changing the Face of the Mountain

Once upon a time in a remote unfriendly village called Kamamusa that clung to the side of a mountain, there lived an old lady called Bibi Tumaini whose habits seemed strange to her neighbors. Since the severe cold kept most villagers crowded together near their fireplaces, they did not cultivate the art of hospitality, and rarely spoke to anyone outside of their immediate families. The frosty and unproductive mountainside beckoned no one towards its slopes, even in the less cold seasons of the year. Only the children climbed the mountain secretly, because their parents had forbidden them. The children always met the old lady. Most of the time Bibi Tumaini was bending over digging a little hole in the ground and dropping a tiny something into it. The courageous children would ask, "Granny, what are you doing?" Her reply was always the same, "I am changing the face of the mountain."

The children grew and most left the village for the big cities. After several years a woman called Mazingira returned to share with her husband and children the harsh environment of her youth. When she came back, Mazingira did not recognize the place of her childhood. The mountainside was ablaze with an assortment of colorful flowers swaying in the gentle breeze. Bushes and young trees lent their foliage as shade to the many children and adults along the foot of the mountain. Families and neighbors gathered and had parties together. They all spoke to each other, laughed and played games.

The woman who had returned stopped one of the villagers to ask, "When did all of this come about? What happened to the unwelcoming and unproductive mountainside of my childhood?" The villager replied, "Do you remember the strange old lady who lived here, the one who would wander up and down the mountainside? It was she who planted all these seeds. She went out every day intent on her sowing — believing all the while that the results would bear fruit." Mazingira recalled the image of this old and bent figure from her childhood. At last, she understood the meaning of those words,
  "I am changing the face of the mountain."

~ Adapted by Sister Joan Marie and Sister Carolyn Masicha – Nairobi Kenya

Contents

Our Ancestry
Page

We Are What Our Thinking Makes Us ---------------- 1
An African Diaspora – The Middle Passage ------------ 2
Some Interesting Facts About Africa ---------------- 3
Map of African Continent ---------------------- 4
African Countries And Territories ------------------ 5
"I Am the Dancing Man" ---------------------- 6
The Baobab Tree -------------------------- 7

Growth and Change

Daisy Symbolism -------------------------- 8
Butterfly Symbolism ------------------------ 9
Adinkra Symbols -------------------------- 10
Sankofa – "Go back to Fetch It"------------------ 11
Are You Ready? -------------------------- 12

Weaving Your Basket

Weaving My Abundant Life --------------------- 13
Living Well is... -------------------------- 14
Your Basket of Abundance -------------------- 15
What Are You Going To Be Doing? ---------------- 16
"Reason, Season, or Lifetime" ------------------ 17
Who Are the People in Your Life? ---------------- 18
Naming Those Who Have Been Important ------------ 19 - 20

Filling Your Basket

Page

Adinkra Principle – Nyansapo "Wisdom Knot"
    Purpose Value Worksheets ------------------------------- 21-38

Adinkra Principle – Owo Foro Adobe "Snake Climbing the Rafia Palm"
    Passion Value Worksheets -------------------------------- 39-56

Adinkra Principle – Ananse Ntontan "Spider's Web"
    Creativity Value Worksheets ----------------------------- 57-74

Adinkra Principle – Nokore "Truth Does Not Hide"
    Authenticity Value Worksheets -------------------------- 75-92

Adinkra Principle – Esono Anantam "Elephant's Footprint"
    Leadership Value Worksheets --------------------------- 93-110

Adinkra Principle – Mpatapo "Reconciliation Knot"
    Harmony Value Worksheets ----------------------------- 111-128

Adinkra Principle – Nkyinkyim "Twisting"
    Life Pathway Value Worksheets ------------------------- 129-146

Personal Mission Statement

Writing Your Personal Mission Statement ------------------ 147

Concise Value Statements ---------------------------- 148

My Personal Abundance Basket ------------------------- 149

"We are what our thinking makes us."
~ Nigerian Proverb

An African Diaspora
Trans-Atlantic Slave Trade Around 1650 - 1860

This African diaspora resulted in movement of people through a variety of continents and countries, and using various methods including captivity and, trade and sometimes with offers of false expectations. Over a period of more than 200 years, between the seventeenth through nineteenth centuries, approximately 12.5 million Africans were taken from their countries and forced into slavery. This portion of the era with slave trade was termed the Middle Passage.

The enslaved Africans came primarily from the west coast and central Africa as part of the Transatlantic Slave Trade by European and American slave traders. While most were taken to the Americas some of the captured were also taken to European countries. Conditions on the ships used for transport were horrific – and inhumane by best description – and more than one million Africans did not survive the passage.

Many of our ancestors were sold and traded at different ports in South America, Central America, the Caribbean Islands and the United States. This movement introduced the African influences in those areas. Our ancestors brought with them the wisdom and knowledge of their homeland and the strength tenacity and resilience needed to withstand the atrocities of enslavement.

They brought with them culture through foods, music, creativity and the art of storytelling to name a few. We are descended from a very rich and proud heritage.

Some Interesting Facts About Africa

Victoria Falls is one of the Seven Natural Wonders of the World!

Africa is the second largest continent in the world covering about 11 million square miles.
The Nile River is the world's longest river with a length of 4132 miles.
Lake Victoria is the longest fresh water lake in the world.
Lac Rose in Senegal has a pink color and is safe to swim in.
Sahara Desert is the largest hot desert in the world.
Mount Kilimanjaro, the world's tallest free-standing mountain, at 19,340 feet.
There are over 2600 species of bird and 1100 mammal species living in Africa.
Ostriches are the world's largest bird and native to Africa.
The giraffe is the tallest animal.
With speeds up to 60mph, the cheetah is the fastest land animal.
African elephants are the largest land animal weighing over 6 tons.
Earth's largest reptile is the Nile Crocodile.
Africa is considered to be the origin of civilization and written language.
More than 1000 languages are spoken in Africa.
There are more than 3000 ethnic tribes in Africa.
Karveein University founded in 859 AD in Morocco is the oldest educational institution.
Sudan, with more than 200, has more than twice the number of pyramids in Egypt.
There is a bar built in a 6000-year-old baobob tree in South Africa.

African Countries

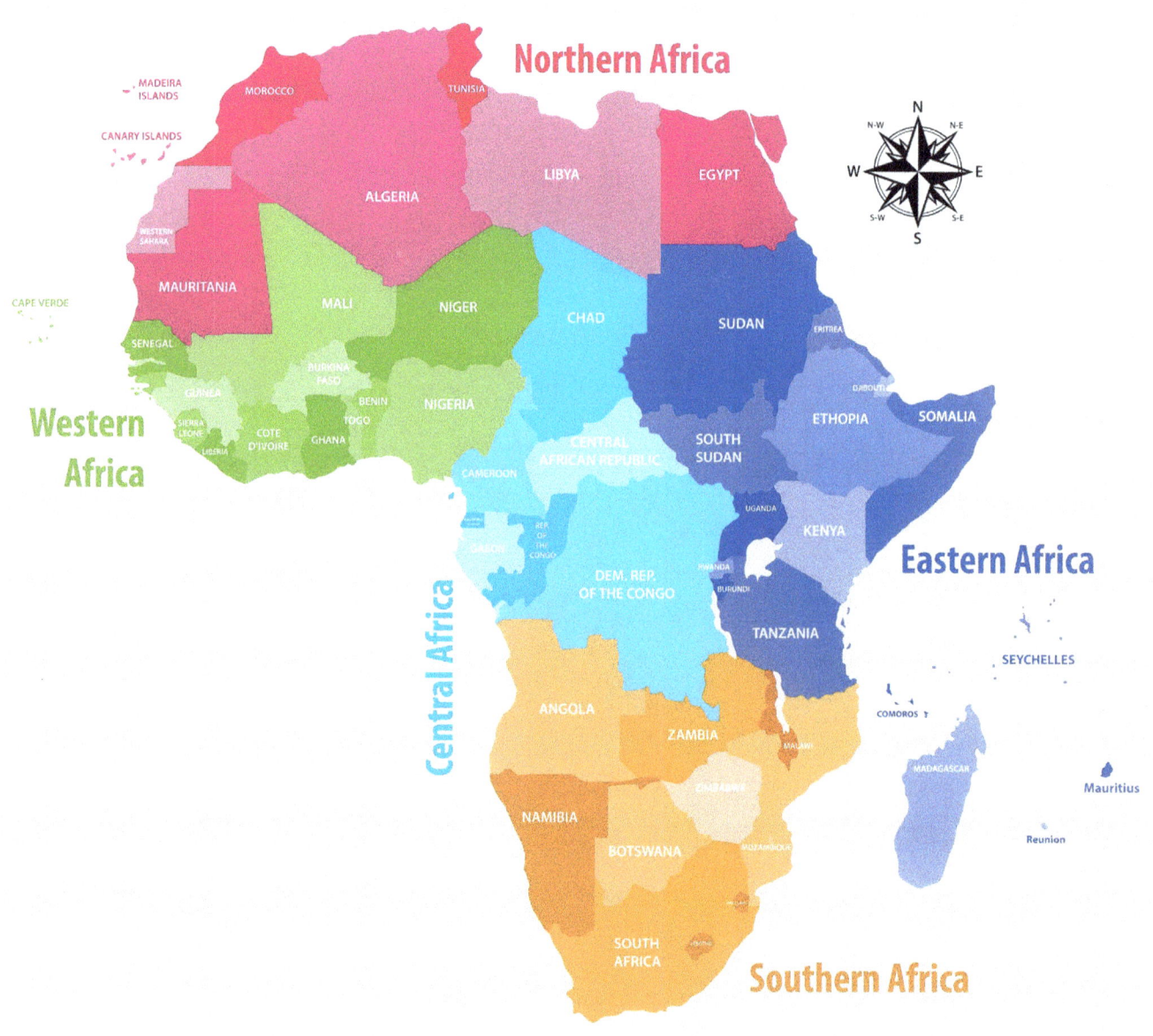

Countries and Territories of the African Continent

Algeria
Angola
Benin
Botswana
Burkina Faso
Burundi
Cameroon
Canary Islands (Territory)
Cape Verde
Central African Republic
Ceuta (Territory)
Chad
Comoros
Côte d'Ivoire
Djibouti
Egypt
Equatorial Guinea
Eritrea
Ethiopia
Gabon
Gambia
Ghana
Guinea
Guinea-Bissau
Kenya
Lesotho
Liberia
Libya
Madagascar
Madeira
Malawi

Mali
Mayotte (Territory)
Mauritania
Mauritius
Melilla (Territory)
Morocco
Mozambique
Namibia
Niger
Nigeria
Republic of the Congo
Réunion (Territory)
Rwanda
Saint Helena (Territory)
Sao Tome and Principe
Senegal
Seychelles
Sierra Leone
Somalia
South Africa
South Sudan
Sudan
Swaziland
Tanzania
Togo
Tunisia
Uganda
Western Sahara
Zambia
Zimbabwe

I Am the Dancing Man

Once in a small village in Africa — Lukulu Village - near the river there lived an orphan boy named Joseph. When he was still very small, Joseph knew that life in the village was dreary and hard. No one laughed. No one danced. But Joseph saw that all around him the world danced. Fire danced near the village huts. Trees swayed in the wind. Clouds danced in the sky. And then, one evening by the river, Joseph met an old man with silver sandals who was indeed "dancing the waves." The old man swept off his hat and bowed. "I am the Dancing Man," he said, "and I have a gift for you." The gift was a pair of silver sandals, and before long Joseph began to dance, taking the old man's place. He danced from village to village, and, as he danced, people responded. An old woman gave him a flower, and Joseph danced with the flower. He met a young child who was ill and in pain, and as he danced the young girl smiled. He met a farmer and saw him sowing seeds. As he danced, the farmer danced as he sowed. Wherever Joseph danced, there was life — until the day came when he was old.

Then one day Joseph looked up and saw standing by the river a young boy waiting as long ago he had waited. The boy drew near. Joseph knew the words to say. He swept off his hat and bowed. "I am the Dancing Man," he said, "and I have a gift for you."

Adapted by Brother Carmine S.M.

The Baobab Tree

"Tree of Life"

Symbol of Life and Positivity

This tree is one of the long-lived plants on Earth known to live longer than 1500 years. The Panke baobab tree of Zimbabwe was the oldest documented tree before it died in 2011 at 2450 years old.

Legend has it that the trees gained their appearance and description as the "Upside-Down Tree" because of the baobab's feeling of being superior to other trees, which eventually prompted the gods to teach them a lesson and uprooted the trees then planted them upside-down with roots in the air to teach them a lesson in humility.

The height of the baobab can reach 82 feet and the trunk diameter 46 feet. Interestingly, the trees can be made of multiple trunks of different ages fused together. The hollow trunks are 80% water, which it soaks up during the rainy season. This storage gives the trees the ability to thrive when all around is dry and parched. Water saved in the trunks is utilized by both humans and animals.

Baobab flowers are white and the petals only open at sunset and are gone by morning.

Fruit grown by the baobab is one of the most nutrient dense foods in the world and has a sweet and citrussy sherbet-like flavor. The hard shells ripen and crack on the tree before falling to the ground when they are dry and ready for consumption.

The African Daisy

Daisy symbolism gives us a feeling of renewal and restores the childlike and simple innocence we tend to lose as we get older. We feel positive, hopeful, happy and grateful for all that we have, both physically and emotionally. The petals of the daisy remind us of the beautiful rays that come from the sun shining brightly. We use that energy to grow and we use the beautiful offerings of the flower to attract others to us so that they too may carry on their life needs.

The word daisy derives from the Old English meaning of "day's eye" because of its unique characteristic of opening its flower at dawn and closing the petals at dusk. This daily awakening and sleeping reminds us of our daily life rhythm. Daisies follow the path of the sun throughout the day to draw in the power of the sun for as long as it can.

Symbolism of the daisy includes:
- *Purity – especially the white*
- *Innocence – the white with yellow centers*
- *Childbirth – often given to new mothers*
- *New Beginnings – refreshing daily*
- *Transformation – new life change*
- *Cheerfulness – positive sunny attitude*
- *True Love – two flowers blended together*

There are thousands of species of daisies in a large variety of sizes, shapes and colors. They can grow and thrive in many different climates. Daisies grow all year round and are naturally resistant to many diseases and pests, which makes them a favorite for many gardeners. Daisies typically begin to flower in early spring, bloom in early summer, and blossom until summer ends.

A single daisy is actually made of two flowers. The center, or flower head, appears to be one piece, but it is actually a composition of many small flowers. Ray florets are the outer part of the daisy and look like typical petals. We too are composed of many layers and facets which all come together to make our beautiful self.

Brightly colored daisies, usually found in South Africa, tend to have longer stems and darker centers, a favorite for florists. The Shasta daisy is another popular type of daisy that was originally bred in California.

Daisies may be some of the oldest flowers on Earth; their images were found in stone carvings dating back to 3000 BC. This flower was grown for medicinal as well as aesthetic purposes. Oils were extracted to use as an astringent to promote healing. Wild daisy tea is said to be useful for throat ailments. Daisy leaves are edible and many include them in their salads. Those allergic to ragweed may also have difficulties with daisy products.

An Illustration of Change

About the Butterfly

Transformation of a caterpillar to a butterfly has long been used to symbolize the process of change in a person's life from one state of being to another. We may find that our current self is no longer useful but the alternative may be unbelievable in appearance and insurmountably difficult to attain. The result, however, is very well-worth the discomfort. In comparison, this transition of a few weeks with a caterpillar may take humans a much longer period of time.

This whole process is called metamorphosis. A butterfly goes through four physical stages in its life cycle. Each stage is very different, and all have a different outcome. The entire life cycle process can take from a month to a year, depending on the type of butterfly.

Stage one begins as an egg. The second stage is a caterpillar after it hatches from the egg. Once the caterpillar has emerged, it is extremely hungry and begins to eat ravenously and grows very quickly. During this hungry stage – from nine to fourteen days – the caterpillar can eat up to 300 times its weight in a single day. The growth occurs so fast that it outgrows its skin, which then must be shed and replaced with new skin. Molting of the skin occurs about four times during this phase. After the last molt, the caterpillar stops eating and prepares to sleep by hanging upside-down from a twig or leaf. Many spin themselves into a cocoon in preparation for the next transformation. Cells within the caterpillar, while it is resting in the cocoon, create the butterfly that will eventually materialize. The emergent butterfly prepares itself to lift through the next phase.

Adult butterflies are pollinators. As they fly from flower to flower consuming vital nectar, pollen grains stick to their tiny legs and transfer between flowers to aid in the growth and development of new flowers.

Monarch butterflies offer an amazing story of the butterfly life cycle. Spring migration of the Monarch begins in March as they head north from Central Mexico. They only have a few remaining weeks to live, and the females instinctively lay their eggs as they move north. North migration continues from March to June and the whole process of 2000 miles takes up to three generations to complete. As winter comes, the butterflies begin preparation for the long journey back to Mexico. Amazingly these new generations of Monarchs know instinctively to travel via the same route of the previous generations.

"May the next few months be a period of magnificent transformation."
~ UNKNOWN

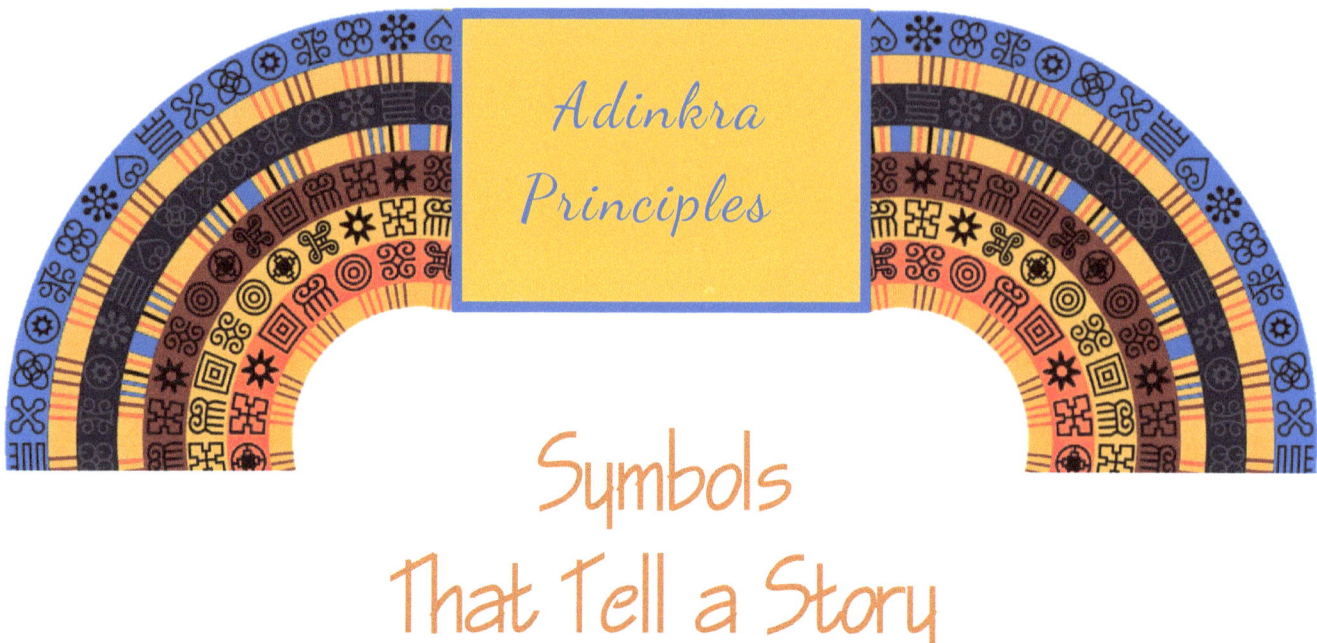

Symbols That Tell a Story

Adinkra is associated with the Asante people of Ghana. The word Adinkra means "Goodbye" or "Farewell" in Twi language. The printed cloths that display these symbols were originally only worn by royalty and spiritual leaders during sacred ceremonies and rituals, especially funerals, to express sorrow and bid farewell to their loved one.

Each of the symbols has a name and meaning associated with it. Some of the images are simple and easy to decipher the implication. Others are more complicated and discovery of the meaning is much deeper.

There are currently hundreds of symbols. They are often connected with proverbial wisdom. Meanings can be connected with historical events, human attributes and behaviors of animals. New symbols are continually added as needed to express new life experiences.

Today the symbols may be worn by anyone and are often seen in artwork, pottery and jewelry, as well as clothing. Adinkra cloth can be worn on festive occasions and gatherings. You may see Adinkra in logos and in product logos and designs.

Traditionally the stamps were carved from gourds and printed on cloth. This process was developed by the Asante people and is a block-stamp technique. Screen printing is also used. Combs may be used to create parallel lines. Dyes were created from extractions of barks and roots. Sometimes the symbols chosen and the design stamp placement are used to convey a message from the wearer to the observer. Bright colors are used for festivities and darker colors for more somber occasions.

Sankofa

(sang-koh-fah)

"Go back to fetch it."

This is the symbol of learning from the past as a foundation for building the future.

In Adinkra symbolism, the Akan believe Sankofa provides guidance for planning our life path. Wisdom from the past builds our solidest future. Past experiences must never be forgotten; instead, they should be used as roadmaps for what is ahead of us.

To hold the privilege to be descended from a continent, which holds a wealth of beauty, culture and wisdom, is such a source of pride. Many argue that Africa is the birthplace of modern humanity. This foundation is solid and worthy of acknowledging as a part of our being.

Despite the adversities we have faced and continue to experience; within us there is an unimaginable strength, ingenuity and determination with an impetus to drive forward.

We have successfully woven the beliefs and practices from a variety of influences into the life we are able to choose for ourselves – If we desire it – and are willing to exert the effort needed to make it come to fruition. With our ancestry, we have a responsibility to pursue all that we can, push beyond and bring others with us. This is the greatest reverence and respect that can be bestowed upon those who came before us. Their sacrifices paved the path to opportunities for all of us. Celebrate and remember them!

Are You Ready?

You are ready to begin weaving your wisdom through your heritage using this Lifebook. It is called a Lifebook because it should become an important part of your life planning process; use it to design your best self at whatever stage of the path you are on. As with our lives, this pursuit is uniquely suited for your needs and desires. The Lifebook is living and growing as you do.

This edition will focus on discovery of your core values in preparation for the next editions which will utilize these values for expansion and moving you forward on your journey. The solid foundation that you set now will assist you in establishing baselines for designing plans and effective goal setting based on the important core values that you will determine for yourself. The focus is listed and summarized below.

Your Seven Core Values

- *You will define what is important to you,*
- *You will decide how you want to express yourself to others,*
- *You will determine the process of acquiring, nurturing and enhancing the attributes of the values you determine.*

You should take your time to carefully look deep within yourself as you complete the worksheets. It is useful to collaborate with a partner to see if what you feel is an accurate portrayal of yourself – a sounding board. The worksheets are intended to promote thought, but not tell you what you should do. The answers for you are within you, ready to be discovered, woven and firmly incorporated in your daily life

You will see reminders often throughout the Lifebook to remember to enjoy the process, celebrate successes as well as challenges: they are there for a reason. Transitions and renewals are not meant to be punitive. Like the dais, each day offers a new beginning to welcome and absorb as the daisy and, just like the butterfly the discomfort will be well worth it leading to the beautiful life you desire.

Living Well Is...

Changing,

Growing...

...and Sharing!

Throughout this Lifebook you will see images of butterflies, daisies, and baskets in addition to Adinkra Symbols.

This is to remind us of the unique challenges and beauty they each symbolize – and how past, present, and future is interwoven into the different seasons of our lives, as we move toward creating the image we desire for ourselves.

Your Basket of Abundance

Bese Saka
(bay-say sah-kah)

Bese Saka is the Adinkra symbol of Abundance and Unity and was traditionally associated with the importance of cola nut crops for economic wealth through agriculture and trade.

Wealth of spirit is a different kind of abundance that does not diminish with expenditure. Conversely, this wealth thrives, strengthens and grows as it is put into use and shared with others.

"Sack of Cola Nuts"

In some cultures, baskets are used to safeguard a person's most valued possessions. These baskets may be very intricate and ornate to pay homage to the worthy treasures within. It is necessary that the canes are tightly woven to prevent loss of the important contents. Periodic preservation care is also necessary to maintain the beauty and integrity of the vessel.

These analogies offer a way of thinking as you acquire, utilize and care for your essential guiding principles – in connection with Adinkra symbols and teaching. You will determine for yourself in this section the treasures you hold as necessary and valuable. You will weave your own Basket of Abundance.

We all have an internal moral compass, whose sole purpose is to move our actions back to where we should be when we find we are losing our way. The message may come to us as a nagging nudge that just won't go away or, if necessary, the message may present as an indiscreet shove or shout to get us to pay attention. To redirect ourselves, we just have to be open to listening to and hearing those messages and following the guidance. It is all in our best interest.

The spirit of those messages comes to us throughout our lives. Primarily the guidance comes to us by what we are taught by our influencers and also through our experiences, whether positive or challenging. Influencers may be our family members and friends, but they also may be people we respect and admire as they carry themselves in a manner we desire to emulate.

Our personal world is forever changing, and if we allow ourselves to continue learning, we will grow and polish those core values that make us our best person. If the voice is not always the same, it is because it changes as our principles are redefined. We grow as we know. The process of change is often initially uncomfortable and possibly scary but truly worth it in the end and can become our new comfort.

What are you going to be doing?

To claim and define your seven core principles in this section of your Lifebook, take your time as you go through the activities for each Adinkra Principle. Think carefully about the answers to questions. There is no wrong answer; the right answer is what it means to you. The questions can help you with your journey toward discovery, but they are not meant to tell you what you should do. The intent is to stimulate your thoughts about what you want, how you can get what you need and how you can be of best service to yourself and others. Core values design a blueprint for your life. They are necessary for putting action to your beliefs about what is important to you. You may have more than seven values,
but the Adinkra Principles chosen lay a strong foundation for living well. You define how they are valuable to you and how to acquire, nourish and hold them within you.

Work through each principle in the order that works best for you and at the pace that is comfortable for you. You will find recurring thoughts and ideas that connect and overlap the values.
This is because all aspects of who we are should connect to make us whole and complete.

If you have the principle already, think about how it came to you. This can help you in finding your strengths or resources for other areas. If there are values important to you, but you don't yet have the attributes that are needed to bring them into your life, Lifebook activities offer opportunities to think of ways to make them a part of your being. Use the brainstorming pages to help you visualize each value in your life and what you need to bring it to reality.

You may find it helpful to partner with someone you trust as a sounding board for what you are finding. Ideally, this person should honestly and compassionately let you know if what you are thinking is what you are projecting as what you desire.

When you have established all seven Adinkra Principles, write your Personal Mission Statement using all seven core values. In your mission, commit to daily employing, enhancing, repairing and sharing something about your principles. All of them do not need to be touched daily but should remain interwoven into your actions.

Knowing where you are going makes reaching your life journey destination so much more exciting and with minimal need for rerouting!

*Most importantly as usual, enjoy the process,
it is not punishment; it makes you better!*

Reason, Season, or Lifetime

People come into your life for a Reason, a Season or a Lifetime.
When you figure out which it is, you know exactly what to do.

When someone is in your life for a *REASON*,
It is usually to meet a need you have expressed outwardly or inwardly.
They have come to assist you through a difficulty,
Or to provide you with guidance and support,
To aid you physically, emotionally, or even spiritually.

They may seem like a godsend to you, and they are.
They are there for the reason you need them to be.
Then, without any wrong doing on your part or at an inconvenient time,
This person will say or do something to bring the relationship to an end.

Sometimes they die. Sometimes they just walk away.
Sometimes they act up and force you to take a stand.
What we must realize is that our need has been met,
our desire fulfilled; their work is done.
The prayer you sent up has been answered and it is now time to move on.

When people come into your life for a *SEASON*,
It is because your turn has come to share, grow, or learn.
They may bring you an experience of peace or make you laugh.
They may teach you something you have never done.

They usually give you an unbelievable amount of joy.
Believe it! It is real! But, only for a season.
And like Spring turns to Summer and Summer to Fall,
The season eventually ends.

LIFETIME relationships teach you lifetime lessons;
Those things you must build upon in order to have a solid emotional foundation.
Your job is to accept the lesson, love the person anyway;
And put what you have learned to use in all other relationships and areas in your life.

It is said that love is blind but friendship is clairvoyant.
Thank you for being part of my life,
Whether you were a Reason, a Season or a Lifetime.

~Author - Unknown

Who Are the People in Your Life?

We often encounter people who have an aura of that "special something" that we admire or draws us to them. The qualities they possess are attractive to us, and we would love to have that same attribute within us. We would love it if they could mentor us – maybe they could if we would only ask!

On the other hand, we may know people who are in roles or positions that we feel are a bad fit for that which they are charged. We witness them negatively impacting our life or the lives of others. We may feel the actions or behaviors of those whom they oversee are not being best served.

Both are examples of influencers that could be beneficial to you for filling your Basket of Abundance. These influencers may be aware of their impact on you, and they may not. Either way their actions add to your personal growth.

Look around you, and seek out those who provide those sparks to becoming your best person, and better yet, use the input to propel you forward with ambition. Refer back to those you identify in the following worksheets as helpful as you work through each of your core values for inspiration.

A major part of the joy and meaning of receiving any life gift is the commitment to share it with others so that the bounty just keeps on giving and growing.

Asking an admirable person for their assistance is not a weakness; it is taking advantage of a growth opportunity. Let them know about the difference they have made within you if at all possible. It maybe an element of their own personal life path to extend what they have to others. You could be helping them grow!

Naming Those Who Have Been Important in Your Life.

Name of Person or Source	R S L	Description of Influence	Aware?

The influencers came into your life for: R – Reason, S – Season, L – Lifetime

Name of Person or Source	R S L	Description of Influence	Aware?

The influencers came into your life for: R – Reason, S – Season, L – Lifetime

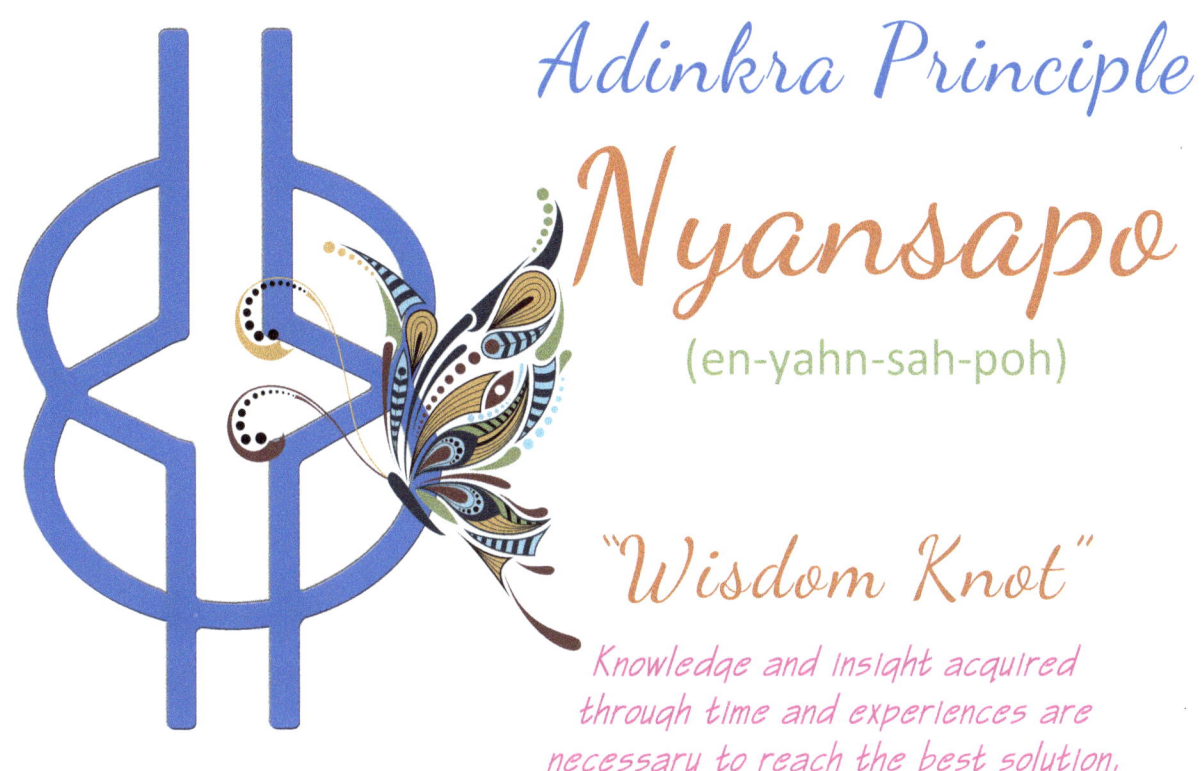

Adinkra Principle
Nyansapo
(en-yahn-sah-poh)

"Wisdom Knot"

Knowledge and insight acquired through time and experiences are necessary to reach the best solution.

Purpose

Wisdom acquired through experiences provides the ability to unravel difficulties and make things right. Force only tightens the knot and makes getting to the solution even more impossible. Patience is needed to evaluate what needs to happen. As you see the tangle loosen, you get a rush of excitement and a strong feeling of accomplishment. You have the ability to do this.

If you do not clearly understand your Purpose, you may feel as if there is something missing in your life. You are trying to put together a puzzle, and it appears that the pieces you need to complete the picture do not fit or are missing. You may be asking yourself what it is you are not doing, why you are here, and what is it you are supposed to be doing in service to others.

It is frustrating to find yourself stuck in an unfulfilling situation that you know is not intended for you. You see others around you appearing to be living their dreams and might wonder "Why not me"?

When trying to find your Purpose, it is imperative that you not waste your time comparing yourself with others and fearing how others will react to what you are compelled to do. This is your destiny, and although you can sometimes take others with you, the ultimate destination is yours alone. This is the peace your soul is seeking, and as long as your intentions have integrity, this is a part of your character.

Remain aware of those messages that stir personal emotions for action. You must openly accept your gifts – what you are good at – and be willing to grow as you move along. Sometimes a disturbing experience can create a need within you to set things right. You willingly make sacrifices to ensure that happens. That is Purpose.

How can you pursue your Purpose?

- Visualize yourself reaching your dream
- Reach out to others who can help you
- Try new things
- Push through discomfort
- Investigate the reason for recurring thoughts
- Keep your goals foremost in your thoughts

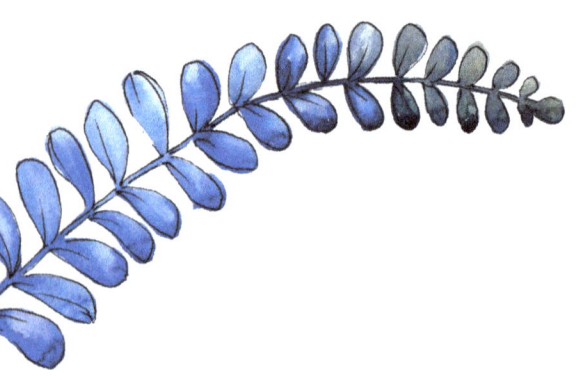

Potential challenges:

- Fear of making a mistake
- Impatience with the rate of progress
- Negative self-talk
- Unwillingness to acknowledge opportunities

Benefits to you:

- You feel great about what you are doing
- You are energized
- Life makes sense
- Creativity is released
- Best use of your valuable time

"Anticipate good, so that you may enjoy it."
~Ethiopian

Wise Words About Purpose

What are the meanings of these proverbs to you?

"He who learns, teaches."
~ETHIOPIAN

_____
_____
_____

"When one is prepared, difficulties do not come."
~ ETHIOPIAN

_____
_____
_____

"You think of water when the well is empty."
~ ETHIOPIAN

_____
_____
_____

"Do not let what you cannot do tear from your hands what you can do."
~ASHANTI

_____
_____
_____

"He who does not seize opportunity will be unable to seize tomorrow's opportunity."
~SOMALI

_____
_____
_____

"When I think of the other's misfortune, I forget about mine."
~ ALGERIAN

"Every door has its own key."
~ KENYAN

"A tree is known by its fruit."
~ ZULU

"If while climbing a tree you insist on going beyond the top, the earth will be waiting for you."
~ AFRICAN

"Suppression of hunger leads to starvation."
~ KENYAN

"Knowledge is like a garden; if it is not cultivated, it cannot be harvested."
~AFRICAN

"We should put out the fire while it is still small."
~KENYAN

"One whose seeds have not sprouted, does not give up on planting."
~KENYAN

"Prepare now for the solutions of tomorrow."
~CONGOLESE

"A tree does not move unless there is wind."
~ AFRICAN

Purpose Attributes

Some questions of Purpose that could be worth thinking about...

- What is your happy place?
___
___
___

- What do you lose track of time doing?
___
___
___

- What may be a sacrifice to others, but is not a sacrifice to you at all?
___
___
___

- What opportunities are you avoiding?
___
___
___

- What keeps you awake?
___
___
___

- What is your heart telling you?
___
___
___

- What do you want to leave as your legacy?
___
___
___

- What do you love?

- What is your vision in life?

- Are you living to your full potential?

- What is missing from your life?

- How do you want to achieve?

- Are you navigating your Path?

- Who do you want to help?

- What compels you to help them?

- What can you do to improve the life of others?

- What piques your curiosity?

- How can you make a difference?

- What do you want to learn more about?

- Do you feel trapped?

- What motivates you?

How Your Life Might Be Affected Without Knowing Your Purpose.

- No drive or action
- Disconnect from self or others
- No sense of direction
- Poor life decision making
- Inability to set effective goals
- Low energy
- Not open to possibilities
- Stagnant learning
- Feelings of insecurity

Some Key Words Describing the Opposite of Purpose

inefficiency	triviality	inadequacy	hopelessness	futility
meaninglessness	emptiness	unproductiveness	worthlessness	uselessness
disorganization	lack	unimportance	poverty	inability
inefficacy	insignificance	fruitlessness	idleness	weakness
ignorance	pointlessness	incapacity	need	ineptness

My feelings about not understanding my Purpose

_____
_____
_____
_____
_____
_____
_____
_____
_____
_____

Purpose Value Word Cues

Purpose Definitions
- Expected outcome that guides a planned action
- What something is used for
- Having determination to do or achieve something
- Strong commitment to a cause

Highlight the words that express the meaning of Purpose to you.

hope	craving	challenge
consciousness	influence	vision
mission	ingenuity	dream
determination	substance	intensity
incentive	design	attitude
resolve	heart	initiative
aim	persistence	desire
enlightenment	certainty	inclination
lifework	plan	vision
expertise	devotion	ambition
faith	commitment	service
initiative	visualization	tenacity
cause	destiny	blueprint
thrust	interest	duty
doggedness	drive	grit
spirit	aspiration	instinct
dedication	endeavor	longing
inspiration	direction	reason
awareness	fortitude	character
motion	inclination	enjoyment
essence	obligation	message
entrepreneurship	decision	connection
assignment	responsibility	foundation
vocation	concern	pleasure
pursuit	necessity	mastery

Now go back and choose the five _most meaningful_ words to describe Purpose attributes you would like to have in your basket and check the leaf beside them.

Describe each Purpose Value you want in your Abundance Basket and why they are necessary for your personal growth and well-being.
Then rate them 1-5 in order of importance to you.

☐ _____

_____
_____
_____

☐ _____

_____
_____
_____

☐ _____

_____
_____
_____

☐ _____

_____
_____
_____

☐ _____

_____
_____
_____

Purpose Weaving Thoughts

What do I need?

Why do I want this?

When can I begin?

Purpose Weaving Thoughts

Where can I get what is needed?

How can I get it?

Who can help me?

Defining Your Purpose Values

Purpose Attribute	If you have the attribute, how and when did you receive it?
	What were the influences that helped you?

Purpose Attribute	If you have the attribute, how and when did you receive it?
	What were the influences that helped you?

Purpose Attribute	If you have the attribute, how and when did you receive it?
	What were the influences that helped you?

Purpose Attribute	If you have the attribute, how and when did you receive it?
	What were the influences that helped you?

Purpose Attribute	If you have the attribute, how and when did you receive it?
	What were the influences that helped you?

Growing and Enhancing Your Purpose Values

Want Value **Enhance Value** *Circle beside... whether you want to add the attribute to your life, Or Want to grow more attributes of the value that you have.*	What is needed to weave the value into your abundance basket? How can you add or maintain the value?
Want Value **Enhance Value** *Circle beside... whether you want to add the attribute to your life, Or Want to grow more attributes of the value that you have.*	What is needed to weave the value into your abundance basket? How can you add or maintain the value?
Want Value **Enhance Value** *Circle beside... whether you want to add the attribute to your life, Or Want to grow more attributes of the value that you have.*	What is needed to weave the value into your abundance basket? How can you add or maintain the value?
Want Value **Enhance Value** *Circle beside... whether you want to add the attribute to your life, Or Want to grow more attributes of the value that you have.*	What is needed to weave the value into your abundance basket? How can you add or maintain the value?
Want Value **Enhance Value** *Circle beside... whether you want to add the attribute to your life, Or Want to grow more attributes of the value that you have.*	What is needed to weave the value into your abundance basket? How can you add or maintain the value?

Making It Happen!

I am doing the work to find my Purpose.

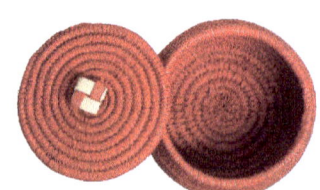

Task	How it will help me.	Start Date	Complete Date - C Or Ongoing - O

Task	How it will help me.	Start Date	Complete Date - C Or Ongoing - O
			C / O _____
			C / O _____
			C / O _____
			C / O _____
			C / O _____
			C / O _____
			C / O _____
			C / O _____
			C / O _____
			C / O _____
			C / O _____
			C / O _____
			C / O _____
			C / O _____
			C / O _____
			C / O _____
			C / O _____
			C / O _____
			C / O _____
			C / O _____
			C / O _____
			C / O _____

My Basket of Abundance
Purpose

I will use the attributes that I have determined to be essential for becoming the person I aspire to be by...

_____
_____
_____
_____

Furthermore, I commit to maintaining the cycle of wisdom by sharing my knowledge with others by...

_____
_____
_____
_____

Adinkra Principle
Owo Foro Adobe
(oh-who foh-roh ah-doh-beh)

"Snake Climbing the Rafia Palm."

Because of its thorns, the raffia tree is a very dangerous challenge to the snake.

Passion

Determination to navigate through what may be perceived as impossible requires a tenacity and true belief that the end result is well worth the risk and discomfort. This guided thrust is Passion. This internal fire fuels you to push past fear and doubt. It feels right.

Have you ever found yourself awakened during the night with a great idea that you need to write down right away while the thought is fresh? Likewise, do you know what you would do, without any thought, if there were no obstacles such as time or money? If you have had these thoughts, you are uncovering your Passion.

Your Passion is what you enjoy doing the most and what drives you well beyond your comfort zone. You are willing to do the work – but it does not feel like work – to learn more and more about it. You are smiling inside and out while sharing what you love with others, and it never becomes tiring.

The cause may be so compelling that it is motivating and it is also challenging, and when you try distancing from the desire, you are continually drawn back to it. The emotional connection is so intense. You are alive, you want to do it, and you are really good at it! Passion is the catalyst for innovation and makes what seems impossible a reality long before it actually comes to fruition. Your senses are extremely heightened.

On the other hand, maybe you feel that you have not discovered what your Passion is. Believe it is there – within you – you just have not recognized it yet. Be patient, keep trying new things, listen to your intuition and be open to all possibilities. Discovery can come anywhere and very unexpectedly. Many facets may come together as one or many Passions can interconnect.

How can you follow your Passion?

- What thoughts awaken you or keep you up?
- Write down driving thoughts immediately
- Seek out mentors
- Truly believe you can make a change
- Partner with like-minded people
- Pursue your interests

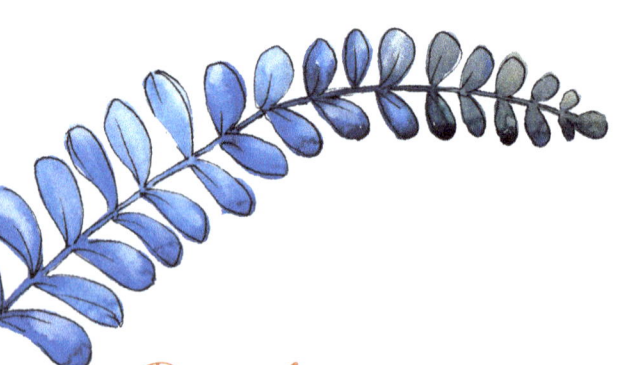

Potential challenges:

- Ignoring those mental nudges
- Wasting your wisdom
- Fear of growing
- Feeling overwhelmed
- Accepting negative messages as truth

Benefits to you:

- You are enjoying life
- Challenges become learning experiences
- You desire to share your wisdom with others
- Others seek you out for your knowledge
- It becomes a part of your being

"Without effort no harvest will be abundant."

~Burundian

Wise Words About Passion

What are the meanings of these proverbs to you?

"Whatever is destined to succeed knows no failure."
~ CONGOLESE

_____
_____
_____

"Let not what you can do tear you from what you cannot do."
~ GHANAIAN

_____
_____
_____

"When you are sitting in your own house, you do not learn anything. You must get out of your own house to learn."
~ GHANAIAN

_____
_____
_____

"No matter how full the river, it still wants to grow."
~ CONGOLESE

_____
_____
_____

"If you are too modest, you will go hungry."
~ CONGOLESE

_____
_____
_____

"Blacksmiths and woodworkers will never suffer from poverty."
~ CONGOLESE

"When the heart overflows, it comes out through the mouth."
~ ETHIOPIAN

"What one deserves is always better than what one has."
~ ETHIOPIAN

"Unless you call out, who will open the door?"
~ ETHIOPIAN

"No person is born great. Great people become great when others are sleeping."
~ AFRICAN

"To one who knows no better, a small garden is a forest."
~ ETHIOPIAN

"He who is being carried does not realize how far the town is."
~AFRICAN

"You must act as if it is impossible to fail."
~ASHANTI

"Those who accomplish great things pay attention to the little ones."
~MALIAN

"Happiness requires something to do, something to love and something to hope for."
~SWAHILI

Passion Attributes

Some questions of Passion that could be worth thinking about...

- What does the world need?

- What brings a smile to your face?

- What are you attracted to?

- What excites you?

- Are you open to new experiences?

- What are your talents?

- What are your desires?

- Do you believe there is something you should be doing?

- What are your dreams?

- What is important to you?

- What are you good at?

- What gives you pleasure?

- What do you wish for?

- What angers you?

🕯 What do you hope for?
_____
_____
_____

🕯 What needs to be set right?
_____
_____
_____

🕯 What would be beyond imagination?
_____
_____
_____

🕯 What makes you feel fearless?
_____
_____
_____

🕯 What are your recurring thoughts?
_____
_____
_____

🕯 What feels right?
_____
_____
_____

🕯 Who would you love to mentor you?
_____
_____

How Your Life Might Be Affected Without Knowing Your Passion

- Feeling lost
- Unsure who you are and where you want to be
- Unmotivated for growth and change
- One day just runs into another
- No enthusiasm
- Feeling fearful
- Feeling negative
- Easily discouraged
- Uncertain future
- Mentally foggy
- Unchallenged

Some Key Words Describing the Opposite of Passion

indifference	coolness	stoicism	frigidity	revulsion
nonchalance	stiffness	inaction	disregard	loathing
apathy	detachment	unfeeling	reluctance	stoniness
reticence	idleness	aversion	antipathy	unconcern
passiveness	negligence	disinterest	coldness	dread

My feelings about not having a life Passion...

_____
_____
_____
_____
_____
_____
_____
_____

Passion Value Word Cues

Passion Definitions
- Intense emotional pursuit of a belief or desire
- Something that creates an intense interest and enthusiasm
- Quest for an uncontrollable urge

Highlight the words that express the meaning of Passion to you.

fire	emotion	fortitude
appetite	rapture	intensity
inspiration	ardor	vehemence
partiality	fierceness	allegiance
craze	obsession	preoccupation
intrigue	insistence	fixation
niche	interest	mission
zealousness	flame	commitment
dedication	aspiration	absorption
hankering	mania	elation
sentiment	devotion	feeling
desire	fascination	momentum
ebullience	longing	adoration
fever	delight	spellbinding
madness	itch	immersion
drive	eagerness	determination
seduction	spirit	loyalty
impulse	fervor	gusto
enthusiasm	stimulation	sensation
initiative	addiction	excitement
yearning	inclination	thrill
ache	thirst	fanaticism
frenzy	doggedness	storm
wishing	enchantment	obligation
exhilaration	zest	impetus

Now go back and choose the five _most meaningful_ words to describe Passion attributes you would like to have in your basket and check the leaf beside them.

Describe each Passion Value you want in your Abundance Basket and why they are necessary for your personal growth and well-being. Then rate them 1-5 in order of importance to you.

- [ ] _____
  _____
  _____
  _____

- [ ] _____
  _____
  _____
  _____

- [ ] _____
  _____
  _____
  _____

- [ ] _____
  _____
  _____
  _____

- [ ] _____
  _____
  _____
  _____

Defining Your Passion Values

Passion Attribute	If you have the attribute, how and when did you receive it?
	What were the influences that helped you?

Passion Attribute	If you have the attribute, how and when did you receive it?
	What were the influences that helped you?

Passion Attribute	If you have the attribute, how and when did you receive it?
	What were the influences that helped you?

Passion Attribute	If you have the attribute, how and when did you receive it?
	What were the influences that helped you?

Passion Attribute	If you have the attribute, how and when did you receive it?
	What were the influences that helped you?

Growing and Enhancing Your Passion Values

Want Value
Enhance Value

Circle beside... whether you want to add the attribute to your life, Or Want to grow more attributes of the value that you have.

What is needed to weave the value into your abundance basket?

How can you add or maintain the value?

Want Value
Enhance Value

Circle beside... whether you want to add the attribute to your life, Or Want to grow more attributes of the value that you have.

What is needed to weave the value into your abundance basket?

How can you add or maintain the value?

Want Value
Enhance Value

Circle beside... whether you want to add the attribute to your life, Or Want to grow more attributes of the value that you have.

What is needed to weave the value into your abundance basket?

How can you add or maintain the value?

Want Value
Enhance Value

Circle beside... whether you want to add the attribute to your life, Or Want to grow more attributes of the value that you have.

What is needed to weave the value into your abundance basket?

How can you add or maintain the value?

Want Value
Enhance Value

Circle beside... whether you want to add the attribute to your life, Or Want to grow more attributes of the value that you have.

What is needed to weave the value into your abundance basket?

How can you add or maintain the value?

Passion Weaving Thoughts

What do I need?

Why do I want this?

When can I begin?

Passion Weaving Thoughts

Passion Weaving Thoughts

Where can I get what is needed?

How can I get it?

Who can help me?

Making It Happen!

I am doing the work to follow my Passion.

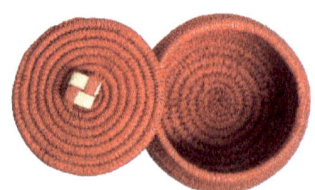

Task	How it will help me.	Start Date	Complete Date - C Or Ongoing - O

Task	How it will help me.	Start Date	Complete Date - C Or Ongoing - O
			C O
			C O
			C O
			C O
			C O
			C O
			C O
			C O
			C O
			C O
			C O
			C O
			C O
			C O
			C O
			C O
			C O
			C O
			C O
			C O
			C O
			C O
			C O
			C O

My Basket of Abundance
Passion

I will use the attributes that I have determined to be essential for becoming the person I aspire to be by...

_____
_____
_____
_____

Furthermore I commit to maintaining the cycle of wisdom by sharing my knowledge with others by...

_____
_____
_____
_____

Adinkra Principle
Ananse Ntontan
(ah-nahn-say en-tohn-than)

"Spider's Web"

The spider is a very relentlessly patient, crafty and industrious creature.

Creativity

Your Creativity comes from those attributes that have been selected just for you. They are the combination of unique skills and talents only you possess. You may already know what they are but have not optimized them. You may also have not recognized what has been gifted to you. You could be overlooking the valuable knowledge you have to help you on your life path.

Your talents come naturally to you. Tasks can be performed with little or no extra effort, and you enjoy doing them. The talent may require enhanced training and coaching to maintain peak performance, but the results for you are very rewarding. Others will see the ability in you. You can discover your talents by expanding your range and trying new things that you may have overlooked as possibilities.

When something just seems to come to you and make sense without really thinking about how it happens, it is a special skill. You can see improvements or different ways of doing things that others cannot even fathom. This is the creative side of you. You can see something in nothing, you are open to possibilities becoming realities, and you have the ability to make it happen. Others are amazed at your end result.

Be aware of what you may be called upon to do based on what others see in you as the right person for the task. The wonderful thing is that it is never too late to acknowledge your Creative gifts. They may appear during challenging situations and manifest themselves in your ability to seamlessly move through the difficulty.

Your Creativity can open doors of opportunity and allow you to access new roads on your life path that were not there before. Creativity is not just for receiving; you have a responsibility to use it and to share with others as well. It all moves full circle.

How can you unleash your Creativity?

- Recognize your importance
- Know what is uniquely special about you
- Expand on skills you have
- Recognize how you influence successes
- Ask other what they see in you
- Take a class in something unfamiliar to you

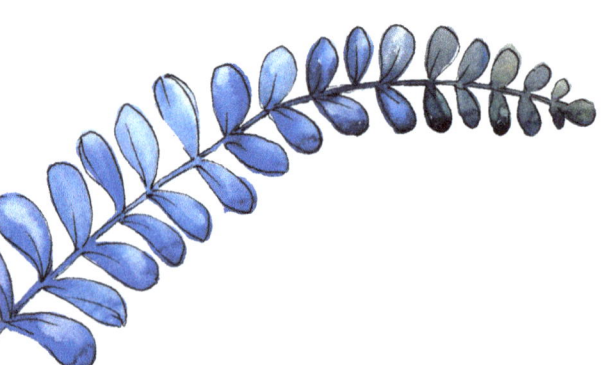

Potential challenges:

- Unwillingness to reach outside of what you know
- Feeling it is too late to start something new
- Fear of failure
- Procrastination with using your talents

Benefits to you:

- Finding new ways of doing things
- You are in action mode for progress
- You are giving to others
- You get out of your own way
- You see things more positively

"A rich man who does not know himself is worth less than a poor man who does."
~Burundian

Wise Words About Creativity

What are the meanings of these proverbs to you?

"If one does not know, another man teaches him."
~GHANAIAN

"Once we have something, do not take it for granted."
~ ALGERIAN

"Never rely on something you do not own."
~ ALGERIAN

"A fool speaks; a wise man listens."
~ETHIOPIAN

"Only the man who says he is not hungry says the coconut has a hard shell."
~ETHIOPIAN

"Before you ask a man for clothes, look at the clothes he is wearing."
~ BENINESE

"What you give, you get ten times over."
~ BENINESE

"God gives, but he does not sell."
~ BURUNDIAN

"Wisdom does not come overnight."
~ SOMALI

"Only a wise person can solve a difficult problem."
~ AKAN

"Knowledge without wisdom is like water in the sand."
~GUINEAN

"If you are filled with pride, then only you will have no room for wisdom."
~AFRICAN

"He who receives a gift does not measure it."
~AFRICAN

"A friend is someone who shares your happiness and your pain."
~ALGERIAN

"You become wise when you run out of money."
~GHANAIAN

Creativity Attributes

Some questions of Creativity that could be worth thinking about...

- How do you learn best?

- What is the beauty in life?

- What comes easy for you to learn or do?

- What things are mysterious to you?

- How do others describe you?

- What are your strengths?

- What have you excelled at in the past?

- What are you known for?

- What are your interests and hobbies?

- How do you handle challenges?

- What do you enjoy?

- Do you connect well with others?

- How can dreams come true for you?

- How do you enjoy spending time?

- How do you motivate others?

- Can you see the bright side of life?

- Do you write well?

- Do you enjoy solving problems?

- Are you a planner?

- Are you detail oriented?

- Are you persistent?

How Your Life Might Be Affected Without Opening up to Your Creativity

- Having strengths that are not being used
- Talents not being used to help yourself and others
- Not reaching you full potential
- Trapped doing things you don't want to do
- Missing out on enjoyable experiences
- Feeling bored
- Feeling of failure
- Underachieving
- Missed opportunities for growth
- Not connecting with positive influences
- Not seeing your Purpose or Path
- Not seeing your uniqueness
- Feeling fearful

Some Key Words Describing the Opposite of Creativity

loaded down	inconveniences	nuisances	limits	burdens
disfavor	limits	bothers	liabilities	obstacles
confusion	constraints	inhibits	encumbrances	fogginess
obstruction	dullness	blocks	scourges	strains
disadvantages	faults	Impediments	banes	failings

My feelings about not using my Creativity...

_____
_____
_____
_____
_____
_____
_____

Creativity Value Word Cues

Creativity Definitions
- Received without special input
- Natural abilities or qualities
- Original ideas put into action
- Seeing possibilities from raw materials

Highlight the words that express the meaning of Creativity to you.

bonuses	charity	invitations
instincts	incentives	accomplishments
freedom	adeptness	cleverness
keenness	sensitivity	souvenirs
abilities	qualities	bounty
remembrances	enthusiasm	graces
favors	smarts	expertise
attributes	character	influences
rewards	largesse	amenities
generosity	keenness	knacks
contributions	artistry	flair
perks	acuity	prizes
support	specialties	resources
aptitudes	considerations	benefactions
indulgence	liberality	privilege
endowments	talents	strengths
pleasures	awards	donations
value	skills	wealth
fluency	blessings	advantage
inclination	pledges	offerings
capabilities	virtue	craftsmanship
sharpness	fluency	usefulness
gifts	worth	brilliance
expression	compatibility	savvy
bequeaths	tributes	generosities

Now go back and choose the five *most meaningful* words to describe Creativity attributes you would like to have in your basket and check the leaf beside them.

Describe each Creativity Value you want in your Abundance Basket and why they are necessary for your personal growth and well-being. Then rate them 1–5 in order of importance to you.

☐ _____
_____
_____
_____

☐ _____
_____
_____
_____

☐ _____
_____
_____
_____

☐ _____
_____
_____
_____

☐ _____
_____
_____
_____

Creativity Weaving Thoughts

What do I need?

Why do I want this?

When can I begin?

Creativity Weaving Thoughts

Where can I get what is needed?

How can I get it?

Who can help me?

Defining Your Creativity Values

Creativity Attribute	If you have the attribute, how and when did you receive it?
	What were the influences that helped you?

Creativity Attribute	If you have the attribute, how and when did you receive it?
	What were the influences that helped you?

Creativity Attribute	If you have the attribute, how and when did you receive it?
	What were the influences that helped you?

Creativity Attribute	If you have the attribute, how and when did you receive it?
	What were the influences that helped you?

Creativity Attribute	If you have the attribute, how and when did you receive it?
	What were the influences that helped you?

Growing and Enhancing Your Creativity Values

Want Value 🌼 **Enhance Value** 🌼 *Circle beside... whether you want to add the attribute to your life, Or Want to grow more attributes of the value that you have.*	What is needed to weave the value into your abundance basket? How can you add or maintain the value?
Want Value 🌼 **Enhance Value** 🌼 *Circle beside... whether you want to add the attribute to your life, Or Want to grow more attributes of the value that you have.*	What is needed to weave the value into your abundance basket? How can you add or maintain the value?
Want Value 🌼 **Enhance Value** 🌼 *Circle beside... whether you want to add the attribute to your life, Or Want to grow more attributes of the value that you have.*	What is needed to weave the value into your abundance basket? How can you add or maintain the value?
Want Value 🌼 **Enhance Value** 🌼 *Circle beside... whether you want to add the attribute to your life, Or Want to grow more attributes of the value that you have.*	What is needed to weave the value into your abundance basket? How can you add or maintain the value?
Want Value 🌼 **Enhance Value** 🌼 *Circle beside... whether you want to add the attribute to your life, Or Want to grow more attributes of the value that you have.*	What is needed to weave the value into your abundance basket? How can you add or maintain the value?

Making It Happen!

I am doing the work to use my Creativity.

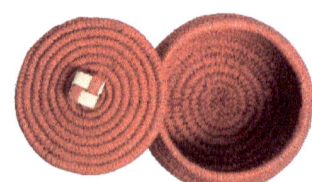

Task	How it will help me.	Start Date	Complete Date - C Or Ongoing - O

Task	How it will help me.	Start Date	Complete Date - C Or Ongoing - O
			C / O _____
			C / O _____
			C / O _____
			C / O _____
			C / O _____
			C / O _____
			C / O _____
			C / O _____
			C / O _____
			C / O _____
			C / O _____
			C / O _____
			C / O _____
			C / O _____
			C / O _____
			C / O _____
			C / O _____
			C / O _____
			C / O _____
			C / O _____
			C / O _____
			C / O _____
			C / O _____

My Basket of Abundance
Creativity

I will use the attributes that I have determined to be essential for becoming the person I aspire to be by...

_____
_____
_____
_____

Furthermore I commit to maintaining the cycle of wisdom by sharing my knowledge with others by...

_____
_____
_____
_____

Adinkra Principle
Nokore
(noh-koh-reh)

"Truth Does Not Hide"

The truth never changes regardless of how we try to change its appearance.

Authenticity

Living with Authenticity involves understanding and open acceptance of who you are and what you represent. The truth is constant and firm. There are no versions of the truth; it truly is what it is. You set the same boundaries and live within what you expect of yourself. You are the designer – not a copy of anyone else. There is no need to apologize for who you are.

When you are Authentic, others see the realty in you and your efforts. Your attributes create an image that is far beyond the average expectation. You have demonstrated that what they see in you is what they can expect with no wavering.

One of the strongest and most impactful commitments you can make to yourself and others is a promise. It gives hope and anticipation as a result of your words. The person given the promise feels valued and assured that you will not let them down. This vow is more potent than *I can*, *I may* or *I will*. Saying *I Promise*, holds power, emotion, connection and Authenticity with the receiver.

Authenticity – truth within yourself – is very sacred and builds self-esteem. You see yourself as worthy of the attention. You are doing something as a result of a strong desire, not because you should – but because you deserve it. Unfortunately, it has been instilled in us to feel guilty for doing things that are making us better. We forget that strengthening our bodies and spirits allows us more means to help others. You cannot give what you do not have.

Inauthenticity breaks the bonds you have established with yourself and others. Consequently, the trust in your words is devalued. This connection may never be reestablished or may remain doubtful and tense. It is therefore vital to not overextend yourself to prevent unrealistic expectations. Sometimes the answer to a request must be no, and that is the sincerest answer that may be given. It is an honest response to what you cannot offer.

How can you show your Authenticity?

- Relationships with others are mutually respectful
- You have integrity
- Live up to your own expectations
- Embrace your life in the moment
- Match what you say to what you feel
- Know what is right for you

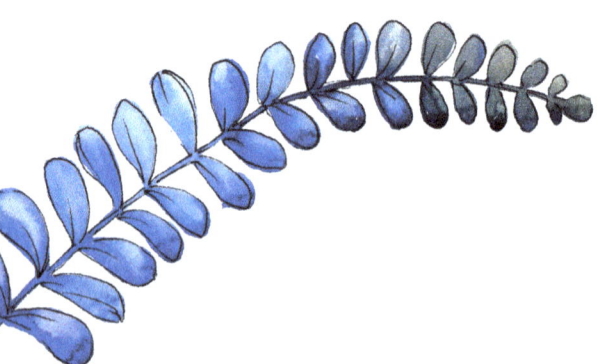

Potential challenges:

- Comparing yourself to others
- Unrealistic expectations
- Feeling vulnerable
- Feeling selfish for taking care of yourself

Benefits to you:

- Self-acceptance
- Living your own values
- Self-discovery
- Confidence in communicating who you are
- Ability to adapt to change

"Examine what is said, not him who speaks."
~Egyptian

Wise Words About Authenticity

What are the meanings of these proverbs to you?

"One falsehood ruins a thousand truths."
~GHANAIAN

_____
_____
_____

"You cannot hide behind your finger."
~GHANAIAN

_____
_____
_____

"He who digs too deep for a fish, may come out with a snake."
~ ETHIOPIAN

_____
_____
_____

"Do not spend an evening in a house where you cannot spend the night."
~ETHIOPIAN

_____
_____
_____

"Confiding a secret to an unworthy person is like carrying grain in a bag with a hole in it."
~ETHIOPIAN

_____
_____
_____

"A good name is better than a good perfume."
~ ETHIOPIAN

"People are aware of their weaknesses, but tend to see other people's flaws."
~ ALGERIAN

"Not to know is bad not to wish to know is worse."
~ AFRICAN

"The teeth are smiling, but is the heart?"
~ CONGOLESE

"If you damage the character of another, you damage your own."
~ YORUBA

"He who does not clean his mouth before breakfast complains that the food is sour."
~AFRICAN

"When the mouth stumbles, it is worse than the foot."
~AFRICAN

"He who tells the truth is never wrong."
~SWAHILI

"It is not what you are called, but what you answer to."
~AFRICAN

"Ashes fly back into the face of he who throws them."
~AFRICAN

Authenticity Attributes

Some questions of Authenticity that could be worth thinking about...

- Do you appreciate those you love?

- Are you kind and forgiving to yourself?

- Are you doing what you love?

- Are there toxic people you need to release from your life?

- Are your thoughts positive?

- What do you question?

- Do you listen to your inner voice?

- Is your integrity important to you?

- Are you living for yourself and not others?

- Does your life feel rewarding?

- Are you open to change?

- Do you really love yourself?

- Are you taking care of yourself?

- Do you laugh and live in the moment?

- Do you enjoy helping others?

- Do you believe in possibilities?

- Are you compassionate?

- Do you celebrate successes with gusto?

- Do you welcome challenging experiences?

- Do you explore and use your gifts?

- Can you face your fears and stretch yourself?

How Your Life Might Be Affected Without Having Authenticity

- Not living your Purpose
- Not living optimally
- Lack of believability and integrity
- Lack of respect from others
- Not being true to yourself
- Not living your dreams
- Frustrations
- No feeling of future possibilities
- Disconnect from others
- Nothing to look forward to

Some Key Words Describing the Opposite of Authenticity

bias	discrimination	indifference	distrust	betrayal
pretense	refusal	hesitancy	prejudice	refraction
denial	infidelity	deceit	hypocrisy	extremism
veto	disengagement	lie	rejection	disloyalty
treachery	falsehood	disagreement	bigotry	severance

My feelings about not being Authentic...

_____
_____
_____
_____
_____
_____
_____
_____
_____

Authenticity Value Word Cues

Authenticity Definitions
- Conformance with reality
- Verifiably accurate
- State of true character
- Indisputably real

Highlight the words that express the meaning of Authenticity to you.

conviction	commitment	endurance
demand	accordance	permission
standing	guarantee	arrangement
aspiration	contract	warranty
affection	optimism	compact
candor	acquiescence	validation
philanthropy	expectation	negotiation
avowal	insurance	achievement
sanction	corroboration	sensibility
bargain	honesty	promissory
oath	integrity	confirmation
acceptance	objectivity	word
recognition	humanity	generosity
concord	agreement	vow
significance	proclamation	affirmation
ambition	capitulation	undertaking
reliance	pact	endorsement
statement	legitimacy	swear
command	approval	obligation
surety	encouragement	assurance
declaration	covenant	hope
anticipation	settlement	dedication
earnest	attestation	requirement
pledge	reassurance	security
buoyancy	receptivity	certification

Now go back and choose the five *most meaningful* words to describe Authenticity attributes you would like to have in your basket and check the leaf beside them.

84

*Describe each Authenticity Value you want in your
Abundance Basket and why they are necessary
for your personal growth and well-being.
Then rate them 1-5 in order of importance to you.*

☐ _____

_____
_____
_____

☐ _____

_____
_____
_____

☐ _____

_____
_____
_____

☐ _____

_____
_____
_____

☐ _____

_____
_____
_____

Authenticity Weaving Thoughts

What do I need?

Why do I want this?

When can I begin?

Authenticity Weaving Thoughts

Where can I get what is needed?

How can I get it?

Who can help me?

Defining Your Authenticity Values

Authenticity Attribute	If you have the attribute, how and when did you receive it?
	What were the influences that helped you?
Authenticity Attribute	If you have the attribute, how and when did you receive it?
	What were the influences that helped you?
Authenticity Attribute	If you have the attribute, how and when did you receive it?
	What were the influences that helped you?
Authenticity Attribute	If you have the attribute, how and when did you receive it?
	What were the influences that helped you?
Authenticity Attribute	If you have the attribute, how and when did you receive it?
	What were the influences that helped you?

Growing and Enhancing Your Authenticity Values

Want Value / **Enhance Value** *Circle beside... whether you want to add the attribute to your life, Or Want to grow more attributes of the value that you have.*	What is needed to weave the value into your abundance basket? How can you add or maintain the value?
Want Value / **Enhance Value** *Circle beside... whether you want to add the attribute to your life, Or Want to grow more attributes of the value that you have.*	What is needed to weave the value into your abundance basket? How can you add or maintain the value?
Want Value / **Enhance Value** *Circle beside... whether you want to add the attribute to your life, Or Want to grow more attributes of the value that you have.*	What is needed to weave the value into your abundance basket? How can you add or maintain the value?
Want Value / **Enhance Value** *Circle beside... whether you want to add the attribute to your life, Or Want to grow more attributes of the value that you have.*	What is needed to weave the value into your abundance basket? How can you add or maintain the value?
Want Value / **Enhance Value** *Circle beside... whether you want to add the attribute to your life, Or Want to grow more attributes of the value that you have.*	What is needed to weave the value into your abundance basket? How can you add or maintain the value?

Making It Happen!

I am doing the work to become Authentic.

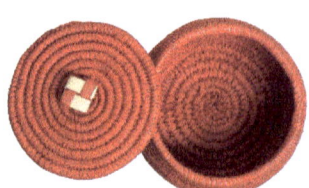

Task	How it will help me.	Start Date	Complete Date - C Or Ongoing - O

Task	How it will help me.	Start Date	Complete Date - C Or Ongoing - O
			C O _____
			C O _____
			C O _____
			C O _____
			C O _____
			C O _____
			C O _____
			C O _____
			C O _____
			C O _____
			C O _____
			C O _____
			C O _____
			C O _____
			C O _____
			C O _____
			C O _____
			C O _____
			C O _____
			C O _____
			C O _____
			C O _____
			C O _____

My Basket of Abundance
Authenticity

I will use the attributes that I have determined to be essential for becoming the person I aspire to be by...

_____
_____
_____
_____

Furthermore I commit to maintaining the cycle of wisdom by sharing my knowledge with others by...

_____
_____
_____
_____

Adinkra Principle
Esono Anantam
(eh-soh-noh ah-nahn-tahm

"Elephant's Footprint"

Symbolizes the nurturing and protective nature of the elephant family group.

Leadership

With Leadership, you have the ability and consent to influence the outcome of events. You are the deciding factor and with that power comes the responsibility for making decisions wisely, with much contemplation as to the consequences of your decision. More importantly, it is imperative that you do not abuse the privilege.

Leadership can also be recognized as your abilities and talents. You have insight to see things as opportunities and not as problems. You are open to suggestions and assistance as needed to achieve the best outcome.

You are in control of your thoughts, emotions, attitudes and actions. You must be honest with yourself and others to maintain your integrity. Powerful people must be believable. Your Leadership abilities inspire others to be their best and to have confidence to face their fears because they have seen the same self-determination in you. When there is something that needs to be done in your wheelhouse; you are the person they look to for assurance.

Life, for you, is viewed in successes and you possess the courage needed to design the life you want to live. You demand setting high standards for yourself. You have the authority for choosing or losing those in your life who mirror your expectations.

If you are powerful, you know your path and how to navigate through the journey. Likewise, you have the humility to acknowledge your mistakes and parlay them into learning and growth opportunities. You make no excuses for what you want and are truly willing to put in the work needed to make it come to fruition. You prioritize your tasks to make the best use of your valuable resource of time.

How can you find your Leadership abilities?

- Determining how you can help others
- Creating a plan to move vision into success
- Honesty and integrity in your actions
- Confidence in guiding others
- Ability to inspire yourself and others
- Commitment to see a task to completion

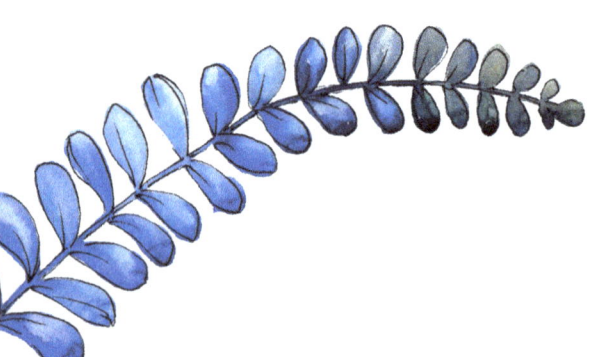

Potential challenges:

- Misuse of your authority
- Disconnection from others
- Lack of empathy
- Inability to accept differing perspectives and input

Benefits to you:

- Respect for yourself and others
- Organizational skills
- Self-assuredness
- Communication skills
- Accountability

"When spider webs unite, they can tie up a lion."
~Ethiopian

Wise Words of Leadership

What are the meanings of these proverbs to you?

"One tree can not be a forest."
~GHANAIAN

_____
_____
_____

"Hurrying and worrying are not the same as strength."
~ NIGERIAN

_____
_____
_____

"A man who pays respect to the great paves the way for his own greatness."
~ GHANAIAN

_____
_____
_____

"One hand can not applaud."
~ALGERIAN

_____
_____
_____

"Eat when the food is ready; speak when the time is right."
~ETHIOPIAN

_____
_____
_____

"The frog wanted to be as big as the elephant and burst."
~ ETHIOPIAN

"Great men have great hearts."
~ ETHIOPIAN

"A single bracelet does not jingle."
~ CONGOLESE

"When you stay with a careless person, you end up becoming careless just like him."
~BURUNDIAN

"He who dictates separates himself from others."
~SOMALI

"To lead is not to run roughshod over other people."
~KENYAN

"The axe forgets, but the tree remembers."
~AFRICAN

"A leader who does not take advice is not a leader."
~KENYAN

"Unity is strength; division is weakness."
~SWAHILI

"If you want to go quickly go alone. If you want to go far go together."
~AFRICAN

Leadership Attributes

Some questions of Leadership that could be worth thinking about...

- Do you encourage respect for the rights of others?
___

- Do you possess leadership skills?
___

- Can you forgive someone when they hurt you?
___

- Can you recognize opposing viewpoints?
___

- Can you rise above your fears?
___

- Are you persistent when you want to accomplish a task?
___

- Are you believable?
___

- Do you appreciate what is given to you?

- How flexible are you?

- Can you see the humor in difficulties?

- Are you connected to a belief in a higher power?

- Are you creative?

- Is learning exciting?

- How do you accept compliments?

🔸 Are you prudent?
___

🔸 Do you have self-control?
___

🔸 Do you enjoy being with nature?
___

🔸 Do you bring energy into situations?
___

🔸 Are you kind to yourself and others?
___

🔸 How do you react to impulses?
___

🔸 Do you manage your time well?
___

How Your Life Might Be Affected Without Knowing Your Leadership

- Feeling chaotic
- Unable to forgive self and others
- Not feeling connected with a group
- Feeling you have no rights
- Inability to see things from different sides
- Unhealthy relationships
- Poor self-care
- Lack of coping skills
- Lack of integrity with others
- Inability to stand up for beliefs
- Poor self-control
- Not feeling driven

Some Key Words Describing the Opposite of Leadership

inability	impairment	sluggishness	incompetence	stiffness
inflexibility	surrender	condescension	laziness	inaptitude
negativity	incapacity	inadequacy	frailty	disdain
obstinacy	vulnerability	weakness	Insufficiency	snobbery
arrogance	inferiority	rigidity	paralysis	stubbornness

My feelings about not using my Leadership abilities...

_____
_____
_____
_____
_____
_____
_____
_____

Leadership Value Word Cues

Leadership Definitions
- Director with influence over a group
- Qualities needed to do something or get something done
- Ability to encourage others to complete tasks
- Authority or persuasive abilities

Highlight the words that express the meaning of Leadership to you.

determination	effectiveness	bravery
existence	flair	competence
impulse	propulsion	entrustment
dynamism	clout	character
inner force	hunger	adeptness
action	inventiveness	force
capability	efficacy	dignity
buoyancy	magnetism	insight
mission	impelling force	effervescence
diligence	expertise	charge
opportunity	amplitude	mandate
energy	flexibility	flame
qualification	fervency	obligation
birthright	fortitude	authority
perseverance	intelligence	stamina
fire	direction	finesse
potency	mastery	boldness
ardency	versatility	intensity
steam	inertia	drive
capability	privilege	dynamism
push	audacity	influence
genius	momentum	courage
determination	endurance	adaptability
personage	responsibility	heartiness
fuel	stalwartness	domination

Now go back and choose the five *most meaningful* words to describe Leadership attributes you would like to have in your basket and check the leaf beside them.

102

Describe each Leadership Value you want in your Abundance Basket and why they are necessary for your personal growth and well-being. Then rate them 1-5 in order of importance to you.

☐ _____

_____
_____
_____
_____

☐ _____

_____
_____
_____
_____

☐ _____

_____
_____
_____
_____

☐ _____

_____
_____
_____
_____

☐ _____

_____
_____
_____
_____

Leadership Weaving Thoughts

What do I need?

Why do I want this?

When can I begin?

Leadership Weaving Thoughts

Where can I get what is needed?

How can I get it?

Who can help me?

Defining Your Leadership Values

Leadership Attribute	If you have the attribute, how and when did you receive it?
	What were the influences that helped you?

Leadership Attribute	If you have the attribute, how and when did you receive it?
	What were the influences that helped you?

Leadership Attribute	If you have the attribute, how and when did you receive it?
	What were the influences that helped you?

Leadership Attribute	If you have the attribute, how and when did you receive it?
	What were the influences that helped you?

Leadership Attribute	If you have the attribute, how and when did you receive it?
	What were the influences that helped you?

Growing and Enhancing Your Leadership Values

Want Value / Enhance Value
Circle beside... whether you want to add the attribute to your life, Or Want to grow more attributes of the value that you have.

What is needed to weave the value into your abundance basket?

How can you add or maintain the value?

Want Value / Enhance Value
Circle beside... whether you want to add the attribute to your life, Or Want to grow more attributes of the value that you have.

What is needed to weave the value into your abundance basket?

How can you add or maintain the value?

Want Value / Enhance Value
Circle beside... whether you want to add the attribute to your life, Or Want to grow more attributes of the value that you have.

What is needed to weave the value into your abundance basket?

How can you add or maintain the value?

Want Value / Enhance Value
Circle beside... whether you want to add the attribute to your life, Or Want to grow more attributes of the value that you have.

What is needed to weave the value into your abundance basket?

How can you add or maintain the value?

Want Value / Enhance Value
Circle beside... whether you want to add the attribute to your life, Or Want to grow more attributes of the value that you have.

What is needed to weave the value into your abundance basket?

How can you add or maintain the value?

Making It Happen!

I am doing the work to develop my Leadership.

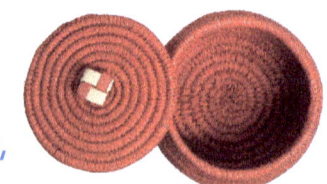

Task	How it will help me.	Start Date	Complete Date - C Or Ongoing - O

Task	How it will help me.	Start Date	Complete Date - C Or Ongoing - O
			C O _____
			C O _____
			C O _____
			C O _____
			C O _____
			C O _____
			C O _____
			C O _____
			C O _____
			C O _____
			C O _____
			C O _____
			C O _____
			C O _____
			C O _____
			C O _____
			C O _____
			C O _____
			C O _____
			C O _____
			C O _____
			C O _____

My Basket of Abundance
Leadership

I will use the attributes that I have determined to be essential for becoming the person I aspire to be by...

_____
_____
_____
_____

Furthermore I commit to maintaining the cycle of wisdom by sharing my knowledge with others by...

_____
_____
_____
_____

Adinkra Principle
Mpatapo
(em-pah-tah-poh)

"Reconciliation Knot"

Creating a bond that results in a mutually peaceful and beneficial ending.

Harmony

There may certainly be physical conflicts and inequalities that require intervention to diffuse real and potential dangers. However, the reality is more often that the disquiet that is felt is a perception of the mind. Conflicts are invited into the thought process. As a situation presents, there is a determination made that something must be done to correct it.

The best arsenal for Harmony is to equip yourself with tools needed to return to a calm and restful state of mind. Simply living can feel as if you are continually barraged with influencers who are determined to keep you anxious and unable to fully enjoy life.

Begin by evicting the mental tenants in your brain that are not paying rent to be there and are destroying the space. Kick them out of your thoughts so you can begin the remodeling. There will always be stressors coming at you, but being able and willing to abandon that which seeks to hold you down gives you buoyancy and resilience.

Harmony is not a guaranteed constant even when you are doing everything you can to avoid letting in negative thoughts. Remember that you are charged and in control of how you react to the stressor. Sometimes you just have to let it go. It is not necessary to always win.

Sometimes the best way to achieve Harmony is to empathize with others. Trying to put yourself in their mind space allows you to see difficulty from another perspective. Now you can think about how you would expect others to see the situation, if you were experiencing it.

The best defense is to neutralize the offending negative with a positive response such as relaxation, meditation and other comforting measures.

How can you live in Harmony?
- Understand what you want your life to be
- Recognize what is not working for you
- Make needed changes
- Connect with yourself and others
- Be in the moment, not dwelling on the past
- Set emotional boundaries and stick to them

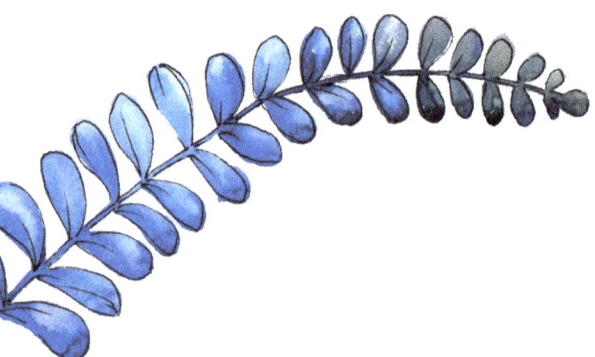

Potential challenges:
- Disorganized environment
- Unrelieved stress
- Inability to let go
- Criticizing yourself and others

Benefits to you:
- Your life feels balanced
- Feeling of satisfaction
- Seeing solutions in problems
- Becoming a part of your personal mission
- Self-acceptance

"Patience is the key to paradise."
~Algerian

Wise Words for Harmony

What are the meanings of these proverbs to you?

"The bitter heart eats its owner."
~GHANAIAN

_____
_____
_____

"It is foolhardy to set a fire just to see the flames."
~ ETHIOPIAN

_____
_____
_____

"As the wound inflames the finger, the thought inflames the mind."
~ ETHIOPIAN

_____
_____
_____

"Evil enters like a needle and spreads like an oak tree."
~ETHIOPIAN

_____
_____
_____

"A loose tooth will not rest until it's pulled out."
~ETHIOPIAN

_____
_____
_____

"If you offend, ask for pardon. If offended, forgive."
~ ETHIOPIAN

"You know who your friends and enemies are during difficult times."
~ ALGERIAN

"A sensible enemy is better than a narrow-minded friend."
~ ALGERIAN

"Do not mend your neighbor's fence before seeing to your own."
~ TANZANIAN

"Quarrels end, but words once spoken never die."
~ SIERRA LEONE

"He who upsets something should know how to put it back together again."
~SIERRA LEONE

"He who forgives, wins the argument."
~AFRICAN

"There is no medicine to cure hatred."
~AFRICAN

"Wood already touched by fire is not hard to set alight."
~AFRICAN

"You cannot hide the smoke of the hut you set on fire."
~BURUNDIAN

Harmony Attributes

Some questions of Harmony that could be worth thinking about...

- How is your health?

- Are you feeling stressed?

- Are you comfortable with being quiet?

- Does your life feel as if it is in turmoil?

- How do you handle conflict?

- Are past experiences nagging at you?

- Do you doubt your decision-making abilities?

- Do you engage in negative self-talk?

- Do you participate in rumors and gossip?

- How is your sleep?

- How are your relationships with others?

- Do you procrastinate to avoid doing things?

- Can you accept things for what they are?

- How do you handle emotional situations?

- Are you comfortable with yourself?

- Is your life guided by to-do lists?

- How do you relax?

- Is your environment and mind cluttered?

- Can you disconnect from technology?

- What makes you feel better?

- Do you get a rush from conflict?

How Your Life Might Be Affected Without Living in Harmony

- Increased worry
- Criticism of self and others
- Can't appreciate the good in life
- Negative preoccupation with the past
- Stress-related symptoms
- Disconnection with inner comfort
- Inability to let go and heal
- Missed opportunities
- Inability to talk through conflicts
- Poor mental focus
- Decreased happiness

Some Key Words Describing the Opposite of Harmony

conflict	agitation	confrontation	antagonism	loathing
hostility	animosity	scorn	grievance	contention
opposition	despair	disagreement	commotion	aversion
rivalry	anxiety	antipathy	fighting	venom
tension	repulsion	uncertainty	chaos	tension

My feelings about not feeling Harmonious...

_____
_____
_____
_____
_____
_____
_____

Harmony Value Word Cues

Harmony Definitions
- Synchrony of actions
- Agreement reached after conflict
- Combination that achieves one accord
- Forming a balanced whole

Highlight the words that express the meaning of Harmony to you.

ease	forgiveness	civil
mercy	composure	goodwill
cohesion	affinity	recovered
recreation	reconciliation	nirvana
fellowship	exhaling	kinship
rejoiced	mediation	agreement
accord	comfort	softness
rest	self-composure	leisure
alliance	happiness	retirement
oneness	security	compatibility
relaxation	symbiosis	symbiosis
contentment	amity	moratorium
joy	patience	symphony
quiet	restoration	bliss
benevolence	calm	consensus
serenity	silence	poise
order	healing	sedateness
cooperation	solidarity	tranquility
reassured	blessedness	assent
sedateness	pleasure	repose
breathing	rapport	stillness
pacification	respite	amicability
stabilized	cooperation	justice
heartsease	unity	organization
successful	soothed	confident

Now go back and choose the five _most meaningful_ words to describe Harmony attributes you would like to have in your basket and check the leaf beside them.

120

Describe each Harmony Value you want in your Abundance Basket and why they are necessary for your personal growth and well-being. Then rate them 1-5 in order of importance to you.

☐ _____

_____
_____
_____

☐ _____

_____
_____
_____

☐ _____

_____
_____
_____

☐ _____

_____
_____
_____

☐ _____

_____
_____
_____

Harmony Weaving Thoughts

What do I need?

Why do I want this?

When can I begin?

Harmony Weaving Thoughts

Where can I get what is needed?

How can I get it?

Who can help me?

Harmony Weaving Thoughts

Defining Your Harmony Values

Harmony Attribute	If you have the attribute, how and when did you receive it?
	What were the influences that helped you?
Harmony Attribute	If you have the attribute, how and when did you receive it?
	What were the influences that helped you?
Harmony Attribute	If you have the attribute, how and when did you receive it?
	What were the influences that helped you?
Harmony Attribute	If you have the attribute, how and when did you receive it?
	What were the influences that helped you?
Harmony Attribute	If you have the attribute, how and when did you receive it?
	What were the influences that helped you?

Growing and Enhancing Your Harmony Values

Want Value / **Enhance Value** *Circle beside... whether you want to add the attribute to your life, Or Want to grow more attributes of the value that you have.*	What is needed to weave the value into your abundance basket? How can you add or maintain the value?
Want Value / **Enhance Value** *Circle beside... whether you want to add the attribute to your life, Or Want to grow more attributes of the value that you have.*	What is needed to weave the value into your abundance basket? How can you add or maintain the value?
Want Value / **Enhance Value** *Circle beside... whether you want to add the attribute to your life, Or Want to grow more attributes of the value that you have.*	What is needed to weave the value into your abundance basket? How can you add or maintain the value?
Want Value / **Enhance Value** *Circle beside... whether you want to add the attribute to your life, Or Want to grow more attributes of the value that you have.*	What is needed to weave the value into your abundance basket? How can you add or maintain the value?
Want Value / **Enhance Value** *Circle beside... whether you want to add the attribute to your life, Or Want to grow more attributes of the value that you have.*	What is needed to weave the value into your abundance basket? How can you add or maintain the value?

Making It Happen!

I am doing the work to live in Harmony.

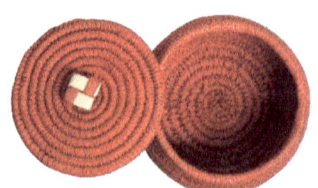

Task	How it will help me.	Start Date	Complete Date - C Or Ongoing - O

Task	How it will help me.	Start Date	Complete Date - C Or Ongoing - O

My Basket of Abundance
Harmony

I will use the attributes that I have determined to be essential for becoming the person I aspire to be by...

_____
_____
_____
_____

Furthermore I commit to maintaining the cycle of wisdom by sharing my knowledge with others by...

_____
_____
_____
_____

Adinkra Principle
Nkyinkyim
(en-cheen-chim)

"Twisting"

This describes the winding and unpredictable nature of life's pathway.

Life Pathway

Your Life Pathway is uniquely yours. Sometimes you may find the direction is not as you thought it should be. Part of getting and staying on the path is remaining open to changes. There may be many twists along the way for the purpose of gaining learning experiences before you converge back to the main path. There may be tests as to how well you are able to problem-solve and adapt to changes. When you know your Life Pathway, you are compelled to move forward at all costs and feel a sense of accomplishment with each leg of the journey.

Knowing the direction helps avoid unnecessary and non-productive efforts. Without insight, you can become frustrated and lost. With knowledge, experience and intuition, some of the anxiety is taken out of the journey. Decision-making and planning become easier, and you avoid wasting valuable and limited resources, such as time and money.

You must be flexible to navigate the unpredictable twists and curves; they are there to teach you valuable lessons. Your interests remain piqued, and they are often small exercises in preparation for something larger. If you allow changes to your routine, the newness creates a discomfort that forces you to challenge and extend yourself outside of ease, and you may be confronted with a different visual perspective.

Challenges are only roadblocks if you allow yourself to see them as such. If you take a wrong turn, remember all is not lost, it may be a message intended to tell you that you need to go a different direction. Watch your step and don't take opportunities for granted. They may not reappear later when you want them.

If you do not know what your Life Pathway is yet, you may help discover it by listening to those inner voices telling you what is important to you and what you need to do to make your personal difference. As always, try new things to find what you enjoy and when you feel a desire to do more.

How can you begin your Life Pathway?
- Listen to your inner voice
- Believe in yourself as successful
- Let go of the status quo
- Evaluate what you are doing or not doing
- Use past experiences to help you
- Pursue your interests

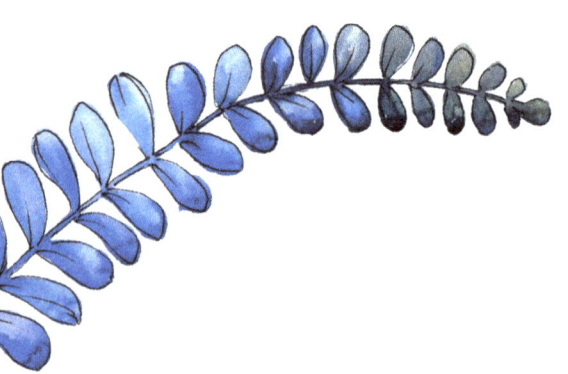

Potential challenges:
- Everyday life occurrences
- Excessive and rigid practices
- Resisting what you know is needed
- Allowing distractions to interrupt progress

Benefits to you:
- You get out of your own way
- Excitement about your life journey
- Adaptability to change
- Ability to create solutions
- Stronger connection with yourself

"If you are on the road to nowhere, find another road."
~Ghanian

Wise Words About Life Pathway

What are the meanings of these proverbs to you?

"No one knows what the dawn will bring."
~ETHIOPIAN

_____
_____
_____

"Thorns prick lightly the man who walks slowly."
~ ETHIOPIAN

_____
_____
_____

"The crow wanted to mimic the pigeon's walk and forgot his own."
~ ALGERIAN

_____
_____
_____

"Experience must always be taken into account."
~ALGERIAN

_____
_____
_____

"Traveling is learning."
~KENYAN

_____
_____
_____

"The best way to eat the elephant standing in your way,
  is to cut it up into little pieces."
~ AFRICAN

"The best trees grow on the steepest hills."
~ BURUNDIAN

"The world is a journey; the afterlife is home."
~ BENINESE

"If you are going to go where corn grows, take a cutting tool with you."
~ ETHIOPIAN

"You may have two legs, but you still cannot climb two trees at the same time."
~ ETHIOPIAN

"If things are getting easier, maybe you are going downhill."
~GHANAIAN

"Do not look where you fell, but where you slipped."
~ GHANAIAN

"It is the path of the needle that the thread is accustomed to follow."
~AFRICAN

"If all seeds that fall were to grow,
no one could follow the path under the trees."
~NIGERIAN

"No one tests the depth of water with both feet."
~GHANAIAN

Life Pathway Attributes

Some questions of Life Pathway that could be worth thinking about...

- Do you manage your time wisely?
___

- Are you organized?
___

- How do you create memories?
___

- What do you do when you encounter obstacles?
___

- What are you waiting for?
___

- Can you rise above negative comments?
___

- Can you see beyond what is right in front of you?
___

- Are you willing to take chances?

- Is your life moving at a fast pace?

- What are your intuitive signs telling you?

- Are you truly enjoying life?

- Are there distractions that need to be removed?

- Are there recurring situations that keep drawing you to them?

- Are you open to trying new ways of doing things?

- Are you maintaining connections with others daily?

- Are you too serious?

- How could you simplify your life?

- Who inspires you?

- Do you like to learn new things?

- Are you flexible with changes in plans?

- Do you take risks?

How Your Life Might Be Affected Without Knowing Your Life Pathway

- Feeling something is missing from your life
- Often feeling ill
- Sense that nothing is going right
- Excessive in behaviors
- Always searching for something more
- Avoidance of uncomfortable situations
- Need to move people or situations out of your life
- Not living up to potential
- Complaining a lot
- Feeling like you're in a rut

Some Key Words Describing the Opposite of Life Pathway

detour	circumvention	blockage	deflection	idleness
inactivity	wrong way	inertia	immobility	motionlessness
substitute	deviation	departure	closure	digression
bypass	lock	exit	stillness	alternate
abstention	stagnation	diversion	inaction	dormancy

My feelings about not visualizing my Life Pathway...

_____
_____
_____
_____
_____
_____
_____
_____
_____

Life Pathway Value Word Cues

Life Pathway Definitions
- A course for conducting life
- Route for moving or traveling
- Direction a person or object is moving

Highlight the words that express the meaning of Life Pathway to you.

process	route	crossing
door	access	journey
road	step	transit
flow	egress	aim
tour	marathon	footpath
bearing	plot	trace
junket	tactic	channel
way forward	bridge	progress
map	locomotion	wanderlust
trajectory	range	transition
freeway	heading	way of life
escape	trail	conveyance
gateway	stretch	plan
travel	voyage	technique
way out	course	mode
conduit	excursion	means
stroll	passage	trip
corridor	highway	race
trek	expedition	orientation
pathway	direction	walk
transport	strategy	navigation
climb	promenade	track
drive	loop	movement
hike	march	approach
circuit	cycle	distance

*Now go back and choose the five **most meaningful** words to describe Life Pathway attributes you would like to have in your basket and check the leaf beside them.*

Describe each Life Pathway Value you want in your Abundance Basket and why they are necessary for your personal growth and well-being. Then rate them 1-5 in order of importance to you.

☐ _____

_____
_____
_____

☐ _____

_____
_____
_____

☐ _____

_____
_____
_____

☐ _____

_____
_____
_____

☐ _____

_____
_____
_____

Life Pathway Weaving Thoughts

What do I need?

Why do I want this?

When can I begin?

Life Pathway Weaving Thoughts

Where can I get what is needed?

How can I get it?

Who can help me?

Defining Your Life Pathway Values

Life Pathway Attribute	If you have the attribute, how and when did you receive it?
	What were the influences that helped you?
Life Pathway Attribute	If you have the attribute, how and when did you receive it?
	What were the influences that helped you?
Life Pathway Attribute	If you have the attribute, how and when did you receive it?
	What were the influences that helped you?
Life Pathway Attribute	If you have the attribute, how and when did you receive it?
	What were the influences that helped you?
Life Pathway Attribute	If you have the attribute, how and when did you receive it?
	What were the influences that helped you?

Growing and Enhancing Your Life Pathway Values

Want Value / **Enhance Value** — Circle beside... whether you want to add the attribute to your life, Or Want to grow more attributes of the value that you have.	What is needed to weave the value into your abundance basket? How can you add or maintain the value?
Want Value / **Enhance Value** — Circle beside... whether you want to add the attribute to your life, Or Want to grow more attributes of the value that you have.	What is needed to weave the value into your abundance basket? How can you add or maintain the value?
Want Value / **Enhance Value** — Circle beside... whether you want to add the attribute to your life, Or Want to grow more attributes of the value that you have.	What is needed to weave the value into your abundance basket? How can you add or maintain the value?
Want Value / **Enhance Value** — Circle beside... whether you want to add the attribute to your life, Or Want to grow more attributes of the value that you have.	What is needed to weave the value into your abundance basket? How can you add or maintain the value?
Want Value / **Enhance Value** — Circle beside... whether you want to add the attribute to your life, Or Want to grow more attributes of the value that you have.	What is needed to weave the value into your abundance basket? How can you add or maintain the value?

Making It Happen!
I am doing the work to follow my Life Pathway.

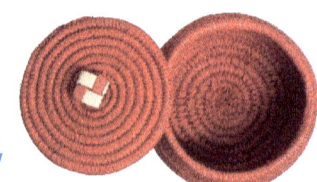

Task	How it will help me.	Start Date	Complete Date - C Or Ongoing - O

Task	How it will help me.	Start Date	Complete Date - C Or Ongoing - O
			C O _____
			C O _____
			C O _____
			C O _____
			C O _____
			C O _____
			C O _____
			C O _____
			C O _____
			C O _____
			C O _____
			C O _____
			C O _____
			C O _____
			C O _____
			C O _____
			C O _____
			C O _____
			C O _____
			C O _____
			C O _____
			C O _____
			C O _____

My Basket of Abundance
Life Pathway

I will use the attributes that I have determined to be essential for becoming the person I aspire to be by...

_____
_____
_____
_____

Furthermore I commit to maintaining the cycle of wisdom by sharing my knowledge with others by...

_____
_____
_____
_____

Writing Your Personal Mission Statement

You have defined the seven core values using Adinkran influences that express how you want to live and how you are going to acquire, grow and enhance them. It is time now to pull all those pieces of imformation together.

Your Pesonal Mission Statement is your introduction to others - whether they already know you or not - as to who you are and what you stand for. It is your personal billboard.

Other people will know the wisdom you possess and aspire to include in you your life. They will see how you will use that knowledge to become your best, and also committed to share with others so that they too may incorporate whatever is useful for them to enhance their lives.

Your Personal Mission Statement clearly and concisely defines your guiding principles and your desire for self-fulfillment. It demonstrates what you believe you have been called upon to do and the choices you have made that align with the values you have outlined.

The statements you proclaim will provide the legacy that will survive you long after you are gone, as to how you personally impacted others by your existence.

All of our lives touch others in varying ways, and those contacts grow exponentially. This dispersion of experiences reinforces the value each of us possesses and the importance of living our best life.

A Personal Mission Statement is a living document in that it gives a snapshot of your commitments for daily living and it also grows as you grow.

This document should be revisited at least yearly, and more often if your needs change, to maintain its value to your life.

To complete this document, go back to the final worksheet for each of your values and write a short sentence that states your intent. Then fill in the areas of the Mission Statement form when you are satisfied with the message content.

Place a copy of your Personal Mission Statement where you can see it daily as a reminder of your plans and how you will use opportunities for living and sharing your values.

Concise Value Statements

- Nyansapo – Purpose

- Owo Foro Adobe – Passion

- Ananse Ntontan – Creativity

- Nokore – Authenticity

- Esono Anantam – Leadership

- Mpatapo – Harmony

- Nkyinkyim – Life Pathway

My Personal Abundance

_____ Date _____

My mission in life is to...
_____
_____

I will achieve this mission by utilizing my identified Seven Adinkra core values as follows:

 Nyansapo - Purpose
_____
_____

 Owo Foro Adobe - Passion
_____
_____

 Ananse Ntontan - Creativity
_____
_____

 Nokore - Authenticity
_____
_____

 Esono Anantam - Leadership
_____
_____

 Mpatapo - Harmony
_____
_____

 Nkyinkyin - Life Pathway
_____
_____

The values I have defined will positively impact the lives of others by...
_____
_____

I commit to daily strengthening my values and thereby optimizing my life by...
_____
_____

Acknowledgements

First, before anything else, I want to thank God for the wisdom and direction that has cleared my path onward, I could not have done it alone.

I am grateful for all the family members, friends, acquaintances, and group participants who have allowed me into their lives throughout my life, and career. You have all encouraged me to learn and share information and experiences, as we all grew stronger.

My daughter, Courtney, and grandchildren, Tavion and Valerie, I thank you for giving me love and smiles. You are such lovely and treasured gifts to my life.

Tom, you have provided me the love and support that you will never fully understand that has made this project possible.

Fern Mann, your editing and suggestions are greatly appreciated as well as the encouragement to keep writing.

Last, and certainly not least, to Jennifer Bright of Momosa Publishing, I thank you for coming into my life at just the right time to help me pull this together and inspiration for me to move forward.

About the Author

A nursing career of more than 25 years primarily in community health education has afforded me the opportunity to learn and share with those who invited me into their lives. My strongest belief has always been a need to listen for the wishes of individuals and to coach them through a self-paced walk of bringing those desires to fruition.

This series of Heritage Lifebooks has been a lifetime in the making as I have gathered the necessary knowledge to add to my personal Basket of Abundance. Sometimes I thought I wanted to depart from my purpose and life path to do other things but I always found myself being drawn back to my personal mission. The departures I have discovered were merely opportunities for me to gain additional valuable information, and they put me back on my journey.

The purpose of the Heritage Lifebooks is so that we may each build our forever home while celebrating our African connection. Home is a place where we feel comfortable, safe, and at ease. Our homes are not just places to eat and sleep, they are places we want to live! A sturdy home needs a strong and reliable foundation to resist damage and avoid collapsing. With *Weaving the Values of My Heritage,* we construct our foundation or assess the existing structure. The most wonderful thing is that we each have what is needed within us ready to emerge for designing our home's most necessary areas. Homes require preventive maintenance and sometimes repairs to keep their value.

Weaving the Values of My Heritage stimulates those thoughts and self-questioning that helps us to access information about who we are, what we desire, and how we can become the people we aspire to be. Usually, we see change as a sacrifice or loss of who we are. We may feel who we are and what we believe are all wrong in comparison to others. The reality is that this is simply not true. Change is individual, and improvements upon ourselves are uniquely individual. Life is for enjoying and making changes is a way better enjoy and appreciate the time we are given and share with others. We create a scrapbook of memories to flip through and smile as we recall the experiences.

I have decided the next Heritage Lifebook, *Gye W' Ani – "Enjoy Yourself,"* is necessary to remind us to remain joyful as we move along the journey of our lives and as we incorporate the values we define in this Heritage Lifebook to become our best selves.

"If you are building a house and a nail breaks, do you stop building or do you change the nail?"

~Rwandan Proverb

Contact me for information
about other Heritage Lifebooks in the series
and companion products,
which support and enhance your discoveries.

Sankofa African Heritage Lifebook Volume 2

Gye W' Ani — "Enjoy Yourself"

Focusing on ideas for rejuvenating yourself
with the joy, laughter, and energy you deserve,
to keep moving on your life journey

Sankofa African Heritage Lifebook Volume 3

Sesa Woruban — "I Change or Transform My Life"

Utilizing your health history and baseline information
sets a framework for determining
what you want and need
to optimally enjoy life.

Sankofa African Heritage Lifebook Volume 4

Pempansie — "Prepared for Action"

Choosing a nutrition and movement program
that fits your wants, abilities, and needs
is important to being able to maximize the benefits
and maintain a lifestyle plan.

Add yourself to the mailing list for availability,
release, and ordering updates.
Group discounts and facilitation supports
are also available upon request.
info@sagesselife.com

Sage4Life
Wisdom for Wellness

www.ingramcontent.com/pod-product-compliance
Lightning Source LLC
Chambersburg PA
CBHW051354110526
44592CB00024B/2977